Prison Decongestion in Nigeria: Challenges and Prospects

Confidence Mbang

Prison Decongestion in Nigeria: Challenges and Prospects

Confidence Mbang

Academica Press
Washington~London

Library of Congress Cataloging-in-Publication Data
Names: Mbang, Confidence (author)
Title: Prison decongestion in nigeria : challenges and prospects | Mbang, Confidence.
Description: Washington : Academica Press, 2025. | Includes references.
Identifiers: LCCN 2025930151 | ISBN 9781680535693 (hardcover) | 9781680535709 (e-book)

Contents

Chapter One
General Introduction ... 1

1.1. Background of the Study ... 1

1.2. Statement of Problem ... 4

1.3. Objective of the study ... 7

1.4. Significance of the study ... 7

1.5. Scope of the Study ... 9

1.6. Research Method ... 9

1.7. Definition of Terms ... 9

1.7.1. Holding Charge ... 9

1.7.2. Legal system ... 10

1.7.3. Anathema ... 10

Chapter Two
Literature Review ... 11

2.1. Introduction ... 11

2.2. Conceptual Framework ... 12

2.3. Theoretical Framework ... 13

2.4. Empirical Review ... 14

2.5. Summary of Literature ... 21

Chapter Three
Holding Charge Practice ... 23

3.1. Introduction ... 23

3.2. The Meaning of Holding Charge ... 23

3.3. The Reasons for Adopting Holding Charge ... 26

3.4. The Procedures that Enabled Holding Charge ... 28

3.5. Justification of Holding Charge ... 32

3.6. Holding Charge *vis-a-vis* the Administration of Criminal Justice Act 2015 and the 1999 Constitution as Amended.................. 35

Chapter Four
The Rights of Suspects and the Effects of Holding Charge.......................... 47

4.1. Introduction.. 47

4.2. The Meaning of Human Rights.. 48

4.3. The Right to Personal Liberty.. 50

4.4. The Right to Fair Trial within Reasonable Time 54

4.5. The Right to Presumption of Innocence 56

4.6. The Right to Dignity of Human Person 59

4.7. The Effect of Holding Charge Practice... 63

4.8. Effect on Speedy Administration of Criminal Justice in Nigeria............... 64

4.8.1. The Effect on the Defense of the Accused Person.................................. 66

4.8.2. The Effect on Nigerian Prison 68

Chapter Five
Summary/Conclusion and Recommendations... 75

5.1. Summary.. 75

5.2. Conclusion 76

5.3. Recommendation 77

Bibliography.. 81

Books.. 81

Journals/Articles 82

Papers.. 84

Internet.. 84

Newspapers.. 85

Chapter One

General Introduction

1.1. Background of the Study

The right to liberty guaranteed in the 1999 Constitution of the Federal Republic of Nigeria is a fundamental right which accrues to all persons. A violation of this right is always taken with utmost seriousness by the Courts of Law. In practice, it has always been perceived that the liberty of a suspect is violated by the law enforcement agencies due to lack of evidence by the prosecution or lack of jurisdiction by the court to entertain the matter. This is made possible by the prosecution filing a holding charge before the court to remand the suspect in custody pending the bringing of a complete charge and evidence for prosecution.

In Nigeria, a critical analysis and census of suspects in custody awaiting trial is alarming and frustrating in the administration of the criminal justice system. In this light, there have been unending conundrum on the subject matter of holding charge. This stems out of the fact that judicial decisions of the 1983 – 1988 has seemed to have made conclusive pronouncement in respect of this matter.

For instance, in 1985 Galadima JCA (as he then was) in the case of *Ogor v. Kolawale and ors*[1] stated thus:

> Before an accused is brought before the court, it should be assumed that the case is ripe for hearing, not for further investigation. He must not be there on mere suspicion under the constitution. If there can be no sensible and prima facie inferences that can be drawn that an offence has been committed, then the accused cannot be deprived of his liberty even for a second. There

---

[1] (1985)6 NCLR 534 at 540.

cannot be a "holding charge" hanging over an accused in court pending the completion of investigation into the case against him.

Also Niki Tobi JSC (as he then was) in *Onagoruwa v. State*[2] had this to say,

> In a good number of cases the police in this country rush to court on what they generally refer to as "holding charge" ever before they conduct investigation. Where the investigation does not succeed in assembling the relevant evidence to prosecute the accused to secure conviction, the best discretion is to abandon the matter and throw in the towel. On no account should the prosecution go out of its way in search for evidence to prosecute when it is not there.

The decisions of the two justices above is pertinent in considering the police usual excuse that investigations are continuing while the suspect is kept away in perpetual detention. It is an indictment to the system of criminal administration and an affront to the course of justice.

However, without prejudice to the reasoning's of their Lordship's, there have been a turn on the tide of authorities by the Supreme Court in *E.A. Lufadeju v. Evangelist Bayo Johnson*[3] reversing the judgement of the Court of Appeal in *Bayo Johnson v. Lufadeju,*[4] which is to the effect that Holding Charge is legal and constitutional in the administration of criminal justice in Nigeria. It is instructive to note that the administration of criminal justice involves three institutions, *viz*: the Nigerian Police Force, the Courts and the Prisons. The Nigerian Police Force is a product of the Constitution.[5] Thus, when a crime is committed, the criminal justice process begins with the police, who have the primary obligation of investigating the criminal act and apprehending the offender.[6] It follows therefore that the police are empowered by the statutes apart from their general duties of preservation of law and order, protection of life and

---

[2] (1993)7 NWLR (pt. 303)p. 49. AT 107.

[3] (2007)8 NWLR (pt. 1037).

[4] (2002)8 NWLR (pt. 768) 192.

[5] Section 214 of the 1999 constitution (as Amended).

[6] R.J Waldron, and others, The Criminal Justice System: An introduction 5th ed. (London. K & M publishers Inc. Routlege, 2010) p. 44.

property, enforcement of law and order,[7] detecting and prevention of crimes also to prosecute criminal cases in court. Thus any police officer may conduct in person criminal prosecution before any court whether or not the information or complaint was laid in by Attorney General of the Federation.[8]

It is also instructive to note that apart from some tribunals established to try certain specialized offences especially during military era in Nigeria, there are perhaps three Level of courts in Nigeria, in which criminal proceedings may be instituted *viz*: Magistrate courts, State High Courts and the Federal High Courts. Of all these it is the police that commences criminal proceedings.

In the Southern states of Nigeria for instance, criminal proceedings maybe commenced in the magistrate courts by laying a complaint before the magistrate whether or not on oath, that an offence has been committed,[9] or by bringing a person arrested without warrant before the court upon a charge contained in a charge sheet specifying the name and occupation of the person charged, the charge against him and the time and place where the offence is alleged to have been committed.[10]

The main objects of these proceedings are twofold. The first is to bring the offender to the court to face his accuser, while the other object as provided in Section 78(b) of the CPA is to bring to the notice of the accused the crime for which he is accused.

Thus immediately a complaint is received at the police station that a person has committed an offence, the suspect is arrested with or without a warrant and brought to the station pending further investigation into the case. At this stage, the police have two constitutional duties to perform in the smooth administration of Justice. They are to grant investigation into the case,[11] or if the alleged offence is of a serious nature in which bail

---

[7] Section 4 police Act, Cap P. 19 L;. F.N 2004.

[8] Section 23 of the police Act op. cit. however this powers have been limited to only police officers who has qualified as legal practitioners, as provided for in section 106 of the Administration of Criminal Justice Act 2015 and section 66 of the Nigerian Police Act 2020.

[9] Section 78 (a) Criminal Procedure Act Cap 41 LFN 2004.

[10] S. Ibid s 78(b).

[11] Section 17 of the C.P.A.

cannot be granted to arraign the suspect in court within a reasonable time,[12] and by constitutional definitions[13] reasonable time is one day where a competent court exists within 40km radius of the place of arrest and in other circumstances, two days as the case maybe or such longer period as in the circumstances maybe considered by the court to be reasonable.

It is pertinent to submit at this juncture that, the remanding of a suspect by the police, either on the basis of lack of evidence or lack of jurisdiction of the court does not in any way breach the provisions of Section 35(5) (a) & (b) dealing with reasonable time, and especially if the charge is held within the further reasonable time as provided in Section 293(1) & (2) – 299 of the Administration of Criminal Justice Act 2015.[14] This is so if done in accordance with the term and tenure of the law.

As a sum up of this issue, there exist arguments as to whether a magistrate can preside on a matter of which it lacks jurisdiction to entertain, and it is accordingly contended that a magistrate has the right to order a remand order for a capital offence. This to me is so because the suspect of a capital offence is better put away from the society than to be left free to perpetrate more offence in the society. The instrumentality of Holding charge is birthed on the theory of crime prevention and this has informed my submissions that, Holding charge despite of all her criticism's is a necessary evil buried in our legal system albeit labelled an anathema.

1.2. Statement of Problem

In the words of Nnamani JSC;[15]

> ... no citizen of this country ought to be detained in any cell (without being taken to a court of law) for more than 24 hours. We ought also to finally turn our backs on the colonial arguments which saw every suspect as a criminal who must be detained.

---

[12] Section 18 of the C.P.A.

[13] Section 35(3) of the 1999 constitution as amended.

[14] Chapter 4 contains a more detailed discussion.

[15] Nnamani JSC, Contemporary Nigeria and Practice of Law, p. 8 Paper Presented at the 1998 Annual Conference of the Nigerian Bar Association held at Benin from 27-31 August 1999.

The terrible effects of pre-incarceration was captured by Galadima J.C.A (as he then was) citing the decision in *Hartage v Hendrick*[16] taken from paragraph 5.2.10 of Apellants brief in *Bayo Johnson's*[17] *case* in the following words,

> The imprisonment of an accused prior to a determination of a guilt is a rather awesome thing it cost, the taxpayer tremendous sums of money; it deprives the affected individual of his most precious freedom and liberty: it deprives him of his ability to support himself and his family, it quite possibly lost him his job, it restricts his ability to participate in his own defense, it subjects him to the dehumanization of prison, it separates him from his family and without trial, it casts over him an aura of criminal guilt.

While those very illuminating words clearly encapsulate the dilemma of Awaiting trial prisoners in Nigeria, this can only be true and accepted if and only if the holding Charge is arbitrarily used or abused. Thus, where a Holding Charge is granted, pursuance and in line with the provisions of the Constitution, and the Administration of Criminal Justice Act 2015 without any extension or breach in time or protocol, then the remand of the suspect is legal.

Therefore, the problem with the subject matter of Holding charge and why it has received merciless criticisms and countdown is due to its use by the law enforcement agencies and the reluctance of the magistrate courts in ensuring that the period of holding the charge is not spent without ordering the release of the suspect. In essence, as we shall see in the course of this work, holding charge is constitutional and legal but it has been left to be like an orphan suffering plethora of criticisms especially from the bench and authors without careful consideration to the reality that it is the mode or manner of it use that results to the breach of human rights, this has resulted to congestion of our prisons (now correctional centres).[18] Research has it that Awaiting Trial Persons (ATPs) constitute a significant

---

[16] 439 P.A, 5684 at (o).
[17] Supra at footnote 4.
[18] Hurilaw, Prison Reform, culled from< https://hurilaws.org/prison-reform> accesed on April 13,2021.

percentage of the prison population.[19] The most challenging aspect is that from the moment those remanded under holding charge steps into the confines of a prison, they are considered "a thing" beyond the fringe of humanity and, conservantly of humane treatment. They are beaten harassed and united with all kinds of indignities and out rages. Moreover, the sprawling prison system of Nigeria is not only infested with myriad of human right violations the entire structures seem, indeed, dependent on these violations for it's very survival in its present, ugly form. Little wonder why Professor Adedokun Adeyemi[20] has described the Nigerian prison system as lacking both deterrent and reformative value.

Finally, it should always be remembered that laws are made for men and not men for laws,[21] the essence of law is to regulate human conduct, protect human rights, while at the same time dealing and punishing offenders in the society. The question that begs for answer is that; considering the present state and well-being of the Judiciary especially the courts in Nigeria, the state of the police and how they typically operate, and the persistent lack of resources and man power in both sectors above, where a person is suspected of having committed a capital offence and he's been detained by the police and there is no practical means of charging him before a court of competent jurisdiction within 24 hours or 48 hours as the case maybe, would it be right and more profitable to the society and Government to willy-nilly allow the suspect to go back to the society? Of course the answer is in the negative, this is because our criminal laws are made to control and prevent crime especially from recidivist. It is the necessity to protect the society that gives credence to the police and courts to remand the suspect of capital offence within the

---

[19] As at early September 2003, the number of ATP discovered between 55% and 75% of the total population of all those incarcerated in our prisons. Out of 40,082 inmates in all of Nigeria's prisons, more than half were awaiting trial, see Uwau M; the prison of tomorrow; a circuit society perspective paper presented at the 3rd summit of shake-holder on the Administration of Justice in Lagos on 17th June 2004. However, by duly 2004, the number of ATPs reached 63% mark. According to a prisons assessment report by the controlled General of the Nigeria prisons service, Mr Abraham Akpe, submitted to the committee on prison DeconYestion, 2,500 prison inmate out of a total prison population of 40,447 are awaiting trial source. Daily independent Newspaper of Tuesday duly 20, 2004, p.E6.

[20] A. Adeyemi, Penal Reform in Nigeria; paper submitted for publication in a new Judicial order. Essays in Honour of Justice Akintola Agunda (unpublished) p.1.

[21] *Per Obaseki in Odi v OSafeli* (1985) I NWLR (pt.1) 17.

period constitutionally and statutorily provided for trail in a competent court of law.

Therefore, it is rightly submitted that Holding Charge is legal but it is the mode of practice that makes it illegal. This work tends to clear the err and popular notion of Holding Charge.

1.3. Objective of the study

The objectives of this research work are as follows:

1. To examine the legal concept of holding charge and remand orders by magistrate courts.
2. To state the constitutionality or otherwise of holding charge.
3. To unearth the nature and operation of holding charge as a necessary machinery in our legal system.
4. To make known the fact that it is the mood of these phenomena that have caused its criticisms
5. To examine the effect of the improper use of Holding Charge to prison congestion and the inhuman conditions of prisoners under awaiting trial.
6. To x-ray case laws and statutes in order to understand the courts view on the holding charge syndrome, and to proffer suggestions on how criminals in Nigeria should be dealt with.
7. To provoke wider thoughts on the proper use and monitoring of Holding Charge.
8. To proffer solutions to all the problems identified during the research work.

1.4. Significance of the study

The study of what the practice of holding charge is, and its effect on the administration of criminal justice in Nigeria is of utmost importance. In numerous countries including Bangladesh, Chad, the Domican Republic, Teuado, El Salvador, Guatemala, Haiti, Honduras, India, Mali, Nigeria, Pakistan, Paraguay, Peru, Rwanda, Uruguay, and Venezuela, unsentenced prisoners make up the majority of the prison population. Such detainees may in many instances be held for years before being judged not guilty of the crime with which they were charged. They may even be imprisoned for periods longer than the sentences they would have served had they been found guilty. This state of affairs does not just only violates human rights norms, it contributes significantly to numerous additional abuses.

The lengthy detention of unsentenced prisoners has its origin in two common phenomena; the denial of pretrial release to criminal defendants, and the excessive duration of criminal proceedings. Both of this ingredients violates international human rights norm.

Solving the problem of excessive pre-trial detention will require courage, innovative thinking, an overhaul of the code of criminal procedure, strengthening the judiciary and in particular, increasing it size and efficiency; provisional release laws and effective substitutes for detention. The precise nature of adopting these reforms will require careful examination and analysis for them to fit comfortably within a country's existing legal framework.

Also the works gives an insight into the reasons why this practice is common among the police. One of the reasons, being delay in carrying out of proper investigation by the police. Admittedly the police force is handicap by numerous logistic constrains such as inadequacy of trained, dedicated and motivated officers. The inadequacy of office accommodation, stationery, transport and communication facilities further limits their efficiency. Transfer of officers handling a case and the lack of transportation facilities to bring prisoners to court constitute additional constraints.[22]

Further, this research goes further to justify the practice of holding charge, affirming its legality and showcasing the improper use of it which is responsible for it loud criticisms.

Finally, the research goes on to provide possible means on modes of the practice of Holding Charge so as to conform with the constitution and statutorily provided time and protocol.

---

[22] O. Agbakoba SAN, Criminal Justice Reform and challenge of Holding Charge, culled from https://www.scribd.com/document/54726488/Criminal-Justice-Reform-Article Accessed on April 13, 2021.

1.5. Scope of the Study

The research considers mostly the legality of Holding Charge *vis-à-vis* the 1999 Constitution and the Administration of Criminal Justice Act 2015, the effects of Holding Charge in Nigerian prisons, the statutory powers of the police and factors militating against the police in carrying out their duties.

The research also looks at the overwhelming necessity of the practice of Holding Charge considering the peculiarity of the Administration of Criminal Justice in Nigeria.

1.6. Research Method

In this research work, the method adopted is doctrinal. In addition, a reasonable number of written materials like workshop papers, journals, conference papers and articles presented in different places and occasion by legal scholars and human rights activists mostly on criminal justice reform in Nigeria.

1.7. Definition of Terms

In this Research work, there are some key words that needs to be elaborate in order to ground better understanding and clarity. It is hereby proposed to define the following key words: holding charge, legal system, and anathema.

1.7.1. Holding Charge

Holding Charge and possibly remand order or detention in custody is part of the pretrial stage in the criminal justice system. It is therefore a charge brought by an applicant usually the police before a court that lacks the jurisdiction to try the matter before it, in order to make a consequential order remanding the suspect pending the advice of the Director of Public Prosecution or Attorney General.

The Black's Law Dictionary[23] define the term Holding Charge" as a criminal charge of some minor offence filed to keep the accused in custody

---

[23] Black's Law Dictionary, West Publishing co Texas; Bryan A. Garner 9th ed, 2009, P.800.

while the prosecutor takes time to build a bigger case and prepare more serious offence".

Jiti Ogunye[24] also holds the view that, Holding Charge is a "term used by the Legal Community in Nigeria to describe a criminal charge that is filed against an accused person by the police before a magistrate court that ostensibly has no statutory power to try the offence charged, but makes an order remanding the person charged in prison custody pending conclusion of investigation or arrangement of the person in the high court upon information being filed by the Attorney General.

1.7.2. Legal system

Generally, the legal system comprises of the whole gamut of the administration of justice system in a society. J. O. Asein [25] said, the Nigerian legal system in the sense, consist of the "totality of the laws or legal rules and legal machinery which obtains within Nigeria as a sovereign and independent African Country". Again Ese Malemi[26] describes it to mean "the laws, courts, personnel of the law and the administration of Justice System in a given state, country or geographical entity".

1.7.3. Anathema

It simply means something which is vehemently disliked by somebody. It means abhorrent, hateful, odious, abomination, bugbear, evil, etc.

Ecclesiastically, a ban or curse pronounced with religious solemnity by ecclesiastical authority, often accompanied by excommunication; something denounced as accursed.

---

[24] J. Ogunye, Criminal Justice System in Nigeria; The imperative of plea Bargaining, lawyers league for Human Rights 2005.

[25] J.O. Asein, Introduction to Nigerian Legal System 2nd ed (Lagos State, Aba press Ltd 2005) at pg 1.

[26] Ese Malemi, The Nigerian Legal System, 4th ed((Lagos; Aba press ltd, 2005) at pg 2.

Chapter Two

Literature Review

2.1. Introduction

The subject matter of Holding Charge is indeed a very crucial aspect of law being that it prevails during the early stage of every criminal offence which pertains to capital offence in situations where the police lacks evidence or where there's no court of competent jurisdiction around the place of the offence. The subject matter is so pertinent and germane in the administration of our criminal justice system, that without it some unrepented criminal will be left free to continue to perpetrate crimes in the society. This fear made the police and courts to confidently uphold the practice in order to save the society. Infact, due to its necessity and inevitability of its instrumentality, it gained more legality and recognition following the enactment of the Administrating of Criminal Justice Act 2015 and other earlier laws of some states.[27] Little wonder why his Lordship WSN Onnoghen Chief Justice of Nigeria (as he then was) in *E. A. Lufadeju v Bayo Johnson*[28] in dealing with the question as to whether a magistrate has power to remand suspect pending formal arraignment at the High Court has this to say-

> A magistrate to have jurisdiction to act there under, the person to be remanded or possibly granted bail where the court has the jurisdiction to so grant, must have been arrested for indictable offence such as treasonable felony which is outside the competence or jurisdiction of the magistrate to entertain. In such a situation the magistrate is empowered upon the suspect being

---

[27] Lagos State Administrative of Criminal Justice Law (ACJL) 2011. <http://lagosministryofjusticre.org.>accessed on April 13th, 2021.

[28] (2007) 8 NWLR (pt. 1037).

> brought before him, to reward the suspect in custody pending the arrangement of such person before a competent court with the requisite jurisdiction to try the said indictable offence.

Mukhtar J.S.C. delivering the led judgment started that,

> The fact is there was strong suspicion that the respondent and some other have committed an indictable offence to wit treason. After their arrest by the police, there was the need to properly and lawfully keep them in custody and the only way to do this was to take them to a magistrate court, who would in turn remand them in custody…

The two excerpts above is present position of the law by the Supreme Court.

But regrettably and pitiable, holding charge has been widely condemned by the league of lawyers, Humans rights activists, authors, jurist, judges and commentator alike, but their position is baseless following the above decision of the supreme court.

However, having noted the trend *vis-à-vis* Holding charge and how fundamental it is to both the safety of the society and human right, this chapter is basically concerned with the conceptual, theoretical and empirical review of holding charge, the theories and empirical review of research works and contribution in respect of the subject, while proffering my observations and submission on the matter.

2.2. Conceptual Framework

The unique concept of Holding Charge is not novel to the practical administration of our criminal justice system in Nigeria. It is an inevitable concept that have come to stay in our criminal justice system, it is *sui-generis* and more of a necessity to the police and magistrate courts. Holding charge is therefore a legal document brought or filed by the police in respect of a suspect or a capital offence where either the police itself lacks evidence to proceed with the case or there is no court of competent jurisdiction to remand the suspect in custody for the duly stipulated constitutional and statutory period, pending proper arraignment for trial. Interestingly this inevitable concept is aimed at establishing the fact that holding charge or remand order is legal and constitutional in our legal system and thus, there is need to clear the erroneous perception of her illegality and as a Lane to our fundamental Humans rights.

Further, the research work shall justify the usage of the phenomena as a necessary evil in the Administration of our criminal justice system throwing more lights on it's instrumentality. The research work shall also proffer a method of her use backed –up with due diligence in order not to breach Human rights. The research work is also important because we shall consider the state of our prison as a result of the improper us of holding charge. The research work shall also authoritatively state the position that a magistrate court need not have jurisdiction to make a remand order. In the words of Prof. Fagbohun,[29]

> It is no doubt that there are already existing blue prints, report and well researched opinion and recommendations on our criminal justice system. While it is common knowledge that our laws in this regard may not have reached its very best, what reappears to be more deficient is not really the law but the machineries through which our criminal justice is administered. The law has taken some steps with some laudable provisions to ensure that a person brought to court by way of a holding charge and remanded in prison custody, is given serious monitoring …

This accords with the earlier views of mine *vis-à-vis* the means of use of holding charge.

2.3. Theoretical Framework

Under this heading the writer proposes to discuss some theories *vis-a –vis* the subject matter. The main theory of the practice of holding charge is the need to safe the society from criminals and the legal incapacity of the police to grant bail to criminal suspect with respect to certain offences. Capital offences like Murder, armed robbery, treasonable felony, rape etc. are serious offence's and punishable with death.[30] However, it should be noted that the underlying Jurisprudence behind holding charge is the need

---

[29] DNL partners, 'Holding charge has statutory and constitutional Basis in Nigeria; <https://www.dnlpartenrer.com/holdingcharge-statutory-constitutional-basis-nigeria Prof Fagbohun/>accessed on April 15th, 2021.

[30] Section 118 CPA, S.35(7) 1999 CFRN.

to preserve the peace of the society by detaining the suspect thus controlling and preventing him from further action. It should hsowever be seriously noted that the seriousness of the police officer in a question for the court and depends on facts. In *Emezue v Okolo,*[31] the court held that offences like attempted murder, rape, burglary, arson are serious offence. For this reason, where the police wish to detain a suspect beyond the reasonable time without being accused of vitiating the 28 or 48 hours as the case maybe, provided by the constitution they have to bring him before a magistrate court for the purpose of obtaining a remand order. The order if obtained will be the authority for further detention of the suspect while investigation into the case last.

In fact, the former Inspector General of Police, Sunday Ehindaro, who before his appointment was a Deputy inspector- General of police and head of legal Department of the police force has written that;

> These are those who have committed or reasonably suspected of committing indictable or non-indictable offences such as murder or armed robbery and the police need them in custody to complete investigation. The law in some states like Lagos and Anamabra provides that such detainee should be taken to a magistrate's court for the purpose of remand.., often times, when the police resort to taking such suspect before a magistrate court pending the conclusion of the investigation the charge is coined a Holding charge.[32]

In many cases, such persons are not granted bail because of the seriousness of the offence. This is the main theory behind the practice of holding charge.

2.4. Empirical Review

In this part, we shall examine some research work done by other researcher's concerning the topic similar to the subject matter. Due to the hardship and result of holding charge in the criminal justice system because of its improper use, the subject matter has suffered merciless criticisms from jurist and text writers alike.

---

[31] (1974) I L.R.N 236.

[32] The Guardian Newspaper on today, duly 15, 2004.

Prof Fagbohun[33] has strongly opined that Holding charge has both statutory and constitutional backing in Nigeria. In his view, the bulk of the challenges confronting the use of holding charges and pre-trial remands are caused by negligent abandonment of pre-trial suspects in prison custody. The professor of Environmental law and Vice-Chancellor of the University of Lagos in his speech, stated that holding charge and detention or remand of an accused person in custody forms part of the pre trial stage of our Criminal Justice System and is a concept which has been widely and erroneously criticized by both the appellate courts and writers.

He said that the totality of the opinions expressed by both writers and lawyers is that holding charge is a gross violation of rights to liberty and fair hearing, but on the contrary both concepts are provided for in federal and state statutes. He referred to the Administration of Criminal Justice Act (ACJA) 2015 and Lagos State Administration of Criminal Justice Law (ACJL) 2011 as well as the constitution of the Federal Republic of Nigeria, and held that the provision now is that a magistrate need not have jurisdiction to make a remand order in respect of same.

He noted that what is needed is rather a reform of the concept and effective use of holding charge as provided for by the law.

Mr. Qudus Mumuney[34] while delivering the keynote address on behalf of the Vice-Chancellor noted that lawyers also share some blame in the unnecessary use of law enforcement agencies to enforce civil and contractual obligation. They noted that it has become common place for lawyers to recover debt in Civil Cases by deliberately writing petition with Criminal coloration to bring same within the jurisdiction of the police who in turn use intimidation, harassment and detention to recover debts. The views of Prof Fagbohun in respect of Holding Charge no doubt, represent the present day position of the law. It is an eye opener to many criticisms that bedevil the subject matter. The view is an obvious adoption of the decision of the Supreme Court in *Lufadeju's case*. The learned Professor of Law succeeded in justifying major challenges as well as making recommendations for Synergy between the courts, Ministry of Justice, the police and the Nigerian correctional centres.

---

[33] Ibid at footnote 29.

[34] He presented the paper on behalf of Prof Fagbohun.

Yekini[35] is of the view, that the decision of the Supreme Court in *Lufadeju v. Johnson* was decided in gross violation and contradiction of the constitution. After analyzing the decision of the court he came into the irresistible conclusion that the Supreme Court decided the cases on grounds of confusion engendered by the applicants, and sentiments for suing the Chief Magistrate in person. He pined strongly that the decision of the Supreme Court was contrary to Section 35 (4) (5) of the 1979 Constitution, Article 6 of, the African charter on Human and people's Rights and Article 9 of the International Covenant on Civil and Political Rights (ICCPR). He concluded thus,

No serious country in the world where human rights are taken seriously allows its citizen to be detained arbitrarily under any pretext, without allowing such a person to face a formal charge before a court of competent jurisdiction within a reasonable time. The author recommended strongly that the Supreme Court should revisit the decision in *Lufadeju* whenever the opportunity arises. He recommended that the court should give effect to the spirit, and letters of s. 35 (5) of the constitution by declaring that the remand proceeding cannot extend beyond the two or three months under any circumstances. Yekini after a community reading of section 35(4) (5) of the constitution, Article 6 of the African charter on Human and People's Rights and Article 9 of the International Covenant on Civil and Political Rights, fell into the error of concluding that the period for remand exceeded the stipulated period of two or three months provided for in the constitution.

Aliyu Ibrahim,[36] is of the view that the practice of holding charge was alien to Nigeria, and the police brought it into bearing as an excuse for improper prosecution. He opined that although the Administration of Criminal Justice Act 2015 which came in force to cure the ills of the defunct Criminal Procedure Act and Criminal Procedure Code has not cured the ills of Holding Charge. He holds strongly that Holding charge is

---

[35] A. O. Yekini, Remand proceedings and the Rights to personal liberty in Nigeria: revisiting Supreme Court decision in *Lufadeju's case*, (Lagos State University Law Journal, Vol VIII, no S. 2 & 3 Dec. 2011/2012).

[36] A. Ibrahim, Decongestion of Nigerian prisons: an examination of the role of the Nigerian police in the application of the holding charge procedure in relation to pre trial detainees.(2019 African Human Right law journal 779-792.

the cause of prison congestion albeit he was sensitive enough to emphasize on the improper use of Holding charge.

Prof Adedeji[37] carried out an exposition of the Administration of Criminal Justice Act 2015, basically Section 293 to 299 and reached the irresistible conclusion that the provisions of the ACJA on remand orders are novel and flow from section 35(4) and (5) of the constitution which requires that a person arrested for an offence should be brought to court within a reasonable time. He cited with approval, the case of *Joshua Idokoigi v Nigeria Police Force & ors* where the applicant was arrested and detained for 5 days. The court stated that steps to keep a suspect further in custody pending investigation must of necessity be done in strict compliance with the provisions of section 293 and 294 of the ACJA by approaching the court within one day of the suspects arrest, for leave to keep him in custody as regulated by the Act, and that any other contrary act must viewed as and declared a breach of the suspects fundamental right to personal liberty.

Again, he cited *A. G Lagos State v Kaite,*[38] where the court held that a magistrate shall have powers to remand such a person after examining the reasons for the arrest exhibited in the request form filled by the police, and if satisfied that there is probable cause to remand such person pending legal advice within the time limit stated in the Act.

He cited the celebrated case of *Lufadeju v Johnson*[39] where his Lordship Niki Tobi JSC at Pg. 28-29, Paras G-B, said, the charge is not read to the accused and therefore no plea taken. That makes the difference between remand and arraignment. Once an accused person is brought under section 236(3) ACJL (Lagos) for remand the magistrate orders his demand without arraignment. By the Subsection, the magistrate can do one of two things; He can remand the accused in prison, he can also grant bail pending arrangement.

He submitted that the ACJA as regards to Holding Charge is a welcome development but that the objectives of the Act will be

---

[37] A. Adedeji SAN, Bail and pretrial detention: pertinent considerations under the administration of criminal justice legislation. (2019 national judicial institute.

[38] (2016) LPELR 40163 (CA).

[39] (2007) 8 NWLR (Pt. 10-37) 535.

considerably realized with the introduction of subsidiary rules to standardize practice and protocols in criminal proceedings. He was very correct in his view after a community reading of the ACJA and the constitution, and strongly recommended for subsidiary rules to effect good and proper practice.

According to Agbakoba,[40]

> Nigeria judicial procedure are plagued with an obnoxious practice, widely known as 'holding charge' whereby the police obtains the endorsement of a court which lack jurisdiction, to remand a criminal suspect in prison custody indefinitely. Suspects held under the holding charge may remain in detention as awaiting trial prisoner for upwards of five years without their cases ever being heard in a court of competent jurisdiction either due to the ineptitudes of the police that cannot conclude investigations, or simply that the case file of the individual is lost.

Agbakoba's view is erroneously predicated on the issue of jurisdiction and this has led to his major criticism of Holding charge. The learned author failed to take Cognizance of the ACJL, ACJA and the Constitution in to bearing.

Also, the Chief Justice of Nigeria, Dahiru Mustapher[41] (as he then was), had his speech read by justice Nwali Sylvester Ngwuta of the Supreme Court at the opening ceremony of the fifth annual general conference of the section on Legal Practice of the Nigerian Bar Association, on 15 November, 2011, where in he stated thus,

> Every legal practitioner is familiar with the term (holding charge) by which citizens are dumped in prison by a court which lacks jurisdiction to try them. It is largely responsible for the congestion in prisons across the country. The state cannot incarcerate its citizen while scrambling for evidence to build a case against him,

---

[40] O/. Agbakoba, Travesty of Justice: An Advocacy Manual Against Holding Charge, (2004).https:///oal.law/travesty-justice-advocacy-manual-against-holding-charge-2004/>accessed on 16th April 2021.

[41] Chief Justice of Nigerian criticizes use of holding charges (Africa criminal justice reform, 2011). Vanguard reports.>https///ACR.org.za/resource-central/chief-justice-of-nigeria-crticizes-use-of-holding-charges.> accessed on 16th April, 2021.

> and if its has a case, it should take the accused to a court of competent jurisdiction.

His lordship continued,

> May I also draw your attention to our prisons where, fellow human beings are reduced to the barest level of humanity. I think time is ripe to include a provision for suspended sentence in the criminal procedure code and the Criminal Procedure Law, after all, as Roscoe pound said in his introduction to the Philosophy of Law (1922), "The law must be stable but it must not be standstill.

His lordship was beclouded by the attendant effect of the improper use of Holding Charge. It is my contention that His Lordship would have rather examined the laws regulating holding charge before finding common grounds to criticize the subject matter.

Mike Ozhekome SAN[42] is of the view that holding is patently illegal and unconstitutional. He argued strongly that holding charge is not known to the Nigerian law and its unconstitutional. The learned also fell into the error of Criticizing Holding Charge solely on the grounds that it is unknown and not mentioned in any provisions of the constitution or statutory enactment in Nigeria. Mr. Femi Falana SAN[43] argue that pre-trial detention is constitutional but holding charge is not known to our laws. On this issue hear him, "The opposition to the pre-charge detention of criminal suspects is erroneously predictable on the belief that it is tantamount to a holding charge, which has been declared illegal and unconstitutional in a plethora of case decided by the court of appeal. Falana is of the view that while a remand order is legal, holding charge is illegal. With due respect to the learned silk I differ on the submission that holding charge is illegal and not known to law. In practice where a capital offence is committed, the police alone cannot just remand him for over 48 hours, rather they file a document praying for a remand order from the

---

[42] Mike Ozekhome SAN, A Holding Charge is patently illegal under the constitution (part 1) Dec. 19, 2015, https://www.premiumtimesng.com/features-and-interviews/195426-a-holding-charge-u-patently-illegal-under-the-constitution-part 1 html accessed on May 3rd, 2021.

[43] Femi Falana SAN, Constitutional Validity of pre –charge Detention of Suspects. February 9th 2016 https://thenigerialawyer.com/constitutional-validity-of-pre-charge-detention-of-suspects-by-femi-falana/ accessed on May 3rd, 2021.

magistrate court tagged a holding charge. It is submitted that the issue of whether or not a remand order is different from a holding charge is just a matter of semantics and must be put to rest.

In fact Prof. Fagbohun's,[44] view is preferable and I agree with him totally. He said thus, "remand or detention in prison custody is the consequential order often made by the court especially magistrate court before whom a holding charge is brought against an accused person. Once the court hears and considers the reasons given by the (police) prosecutor against a suspect on reasonable suspicion of a crime, a remand order may be granted to be held in pre-trial prison custody pending the issuance of the advice of Attorney General or Director of public prosecution".

The learned professor of law continued thus;

> Just like a holding charge, the constitutionality and legality of remanding a person in prison pending the advice of the Attorney General or Director of public prosecution, or pending when the person will be formally charge before a court of competent jurisdiction has been commented on copiously. Mr. Mojosore Onigbanjo SAN in his interview said that "there are many cases. There is *Lufadeju v. Johnson*, there are many and they keep representing it time and time again that there is nothing like remand. A magistrate or a judge of a high court cannot remand somebody in prison. Remand means that you are sending somebody to prison until further enquires are made it is unconstitutional. You must charge him and let him know the charges against Him!!. How correct is this assertion?

I agree with the assertion of the learned professor of law as oppose to the position of Mr. Falana SAN. It can be observed righty that Prof. Fagbohun's position is an improvement and settlement of Mr. Falana's contentions.

In the much cited case of *Onagoruwa v. State,*[45] the Supreme Court held thus,

> In a good number of cases, the police in this country rush to court on what they generally refer to as holding charge ever before they

[44] ibid.

[45] (1992)2 NWLR (pt. 22) 33 at 54.

conduct investigations, though there is nothing known to law as holding charge.

Sec. also *Ogor v. Kowale,*[46] *COP* v. *Anaekwe,*[47] *Enwere* v. *COP*[48] *Johnson v. Lufadeju,*[49] all this cases supports the view that Holding charge is unconstitutional. However, in *Lufadeju v. Johnson* (2007) revering the judgment of the court of appeal in *Lufadeju v. Johnson* (2002), the supreme court held that remanding the respondent in the prison custody by the magistrate pursuant to the holding charge is not a violation of the constitution.

2.5. Summary of Literature

The importance of the subject matter of holding charge cannot be over-emphasized in our *corpus juris*. As highlighted above Holding charge is an inevitable concept that must stay and have come to stay in the administration of our criminal Justice system in Nigeria.

Accordingly, a careful perusal of the forgoing by an objective person would irresistibly lead to the conclusion that holding charge is a necessity and to those commentators clamoring about its illegality and it is rather submitted that it is a necessary evil. We cannot sacrifice the safety and preservation of crime on the altar of fundamental human right if not the society would be a crime recurrent field for humans.

Consequently, with due respect to the various Jurist and commentators on the position that Holding Charge is unconstitutional and illegal, I beg to differ on point of laws and call for a jurisprudential discourse about the subject matter.

---

[46] (1985)6 NCLR 534 at 539.

[47] (1993)4 NWLR (pt. 229) 333.

[48] (1996)3 NWLR 9. Pt 436) 320 at 332.

[49] (2002)8 NWLR (pt. 768) 192 at 217.

Chapter Three

Holding Charge Practice

3.1. Introduction

The police institution is the first institution that a criminal suspect comes in contact with whatever becomes his or her fate will be determined to a large extent by the way the police go about it's duty of investigating and stating the locomotive wheel of the criminal justice system. The police institution is therefore a sieving institution. It sieves, using the barometer role in sieving suspects. Evidence gathering is untidy and more often than not the police are not willing to let a suspect as even when the scale of probable or reasonable cause tilt in his favour. Using the improper use of holding charge the police usually keep the suspect in detention, while evidence of guilt is sought. This improper practice is the main causes of congestion in Nigerian prisons.

Thus, this chapter will focus on the meaning of holding charge, the reason for it's adoption, the procedures of the practice that enable holding charge, the justification of holding charge, and the legality of holding charge which entails holding charge vis-à-vis the administration of criminal justice system and the 1999 constitutions of the Federal Republic of Nigeria.

3.2. The Meaning of Holding Charge

Neither the constitution nor any other existing law[50] in force in Nigeria defines the concept of holding charge. Accordingly, there is no authoritative definition of the term, Ayorinde J. agreed with the assertion

[50] Such as the Criminal Procedure Act, and the Criminal procedure Code.

in *Ogor v. kolawale*[51] when he said that: "our constitution or any other existing law in force in the country does not provide for holding charge…"

One JCA made a similar observation in *Pat Enwere v COP*[52] and proffered the following solutions:

> As the constitution of the Federal Republic of Nigeria 1979, or any other existing law in force in the country does not provide for a holding charge" an accused ought to be released on bail within reasonable time before trail… notwithstanding the absence of any constitutional or statutory definition of holding charge, the practice exist and its improper use portends grave danger to the criminal justice system. In order to capture the essence of the practice, the following definitions will suffice.

A holding charge arises where a person brought before magistrate or Area court for a criminal charge (usually on capital offences) is remanded in prison custody to await commencement of his prosecution. It is the outcome of police inability to investigate and prosecute crime within the time stipulated by law.[53] The practice is predominant in the inferior court of records, particularly the magistrate (in southern estates) and the area court (in the Northern States).[54]

According to the blacks law dictionary,[55] holding charge means a criminal charge of some minor offences fitted to keep the accused in custody while prosecutor take time to build a bigger case and prepare more serious charges. It follows that holding charge is a creation of police prosecutors[56] the intention of the policy is to detain the suspect for as long as investigation into the case lasts including the outcome of the DPP's advice and until there is a final decision or not to take the case to a competent court.[57] Holding charge has also been explained as a charge

---

[51] (1985) 6 NCLR 534 at 539.

[52] (1996) 3NWLR 9. Pt 436 at 320-332.

[53] See section 35(4) of 1999 constitution (as amended).

[54] Towards a Humane prison system. Submission by the civil liberties organization to the Nigerian Human Rights Commission, fully 1996 in Tabiu, M.(ed) (1998), Administration of Criminal Justice Human Rights in Nigeria, chapter five, Pp. 64-74 at P.67.

[55] Black's Law Dictionary, West Publishing co Texas Bryan A. Garner 9th ed, 2009, P.800.

[56] *Anekwe v COP* (Supra) at P.332.

[57] O. Okpara, Human Rights Law and Practice in Nigeria Chengles ltd (Enugu, 2005). P. 164.

brought against an accused person in a court without jurisdiction to try the offence charged pending the receipt of legal advice from the office of the director of public prosecutions for the accused persons trial in the court of competent jurisdiction or tribunal set up to try the particular offence.[58] It is also called remand charge i.e. a charge brought before a magistrate for the sole purpose of obtaining a remand order or where applicable and appropriate, an order for bail.[59]

In order to fully appreciate the instrumentality of holding charge it must be a charge filled by the police or other law enforcement agencies where:

1. A person have been suspect of committing a capital offence
2. There is no court of competent jurisdiction around the place; or
3. The police lacks substantial evidence to prosecute the suspect
4. The advices of the Director of public prosecution have not issued.

The holding charge proceedings are usually instituted for the magistrate courts[60] by police prosecutors. They are common in respect of such heinous crimes carrying capital punishment as treason,[61] murder,[62] instigating invasion of Nigeria[63] and armed robbery,[64] and such other offence is triable by various miscellaneous offence tribunals. The accused is neither expected nor allowed to plea to the charge. Instead the police prosecutor applies the case file to the office of the DPP legal advice. Thereafter the suspect is remanded[65] in prison custody on the order of the magistrate pending a receipt of legal advice.

---

[58] D. Peters, The place of Holding Charge in Nigeria Criminal Jurisprudence. Nigerian Current Legal Problems, (1996-1998) Vol 4/5 p. 256

[59] Ibid.

[60] For various grades and criminal jurisdiction of magistrates about in Nigeria, see generally, Toyin Doherty: Criminal procedure in Nigeria. Blackstone press limited. 1990.

[61] Criminal Code Act, cap 38, LFN 2004 section 37 (1).

[62] Ibid, S. 316.

[63] Ibid S. 38.

[64] Robbery and Firearms (special provisions) Act Cap. P. 11 LFN 2004, S.1 (2). Criminal Code, S. 402.

[65] Remand orders are the usual orders made by the magistrate in a holding charge proceedings, though where applicable, the suspect may be admitted to bail. This is not just because the crimes misused are capital in nature but because the magistrate court concerned has neither jurisdiction to try the accused nor grant bail to him pending trail at the proper forum. See Fidelis Nwadilo, The criminal procedure of the southern states of Nigeria (2nd

Unfortunately, the legal advice may not be forthcoming for a period of a year or more. In the interior, the accused continues to languish in prison custody. Accused persons in this category constitute the bulk of the "Awaiting Trial Men" (ATM). Also when a decision is finally taken to prosecute, the actual filing of information in the High Court or at the appellate tribunal may yet take a much longer period. In all these cases it is the accused whose rights are violently abused who suffers due to the improper use of Holding charge.

Therefore, it need not be further emphasized that Holding charge is a document filled by the police before a court lacking jurisdiction to try the matter, or where there is insufficient evidence for prosecute the suspect pending the advice of the Director of public prosecutor. The product of Holding charge is a remand order.

3.3. The Reasons for Adopting Holding Charge

Having discussed that holding charge is practicable in the Nigerian Legal system, below are the reasons for this practice.

1. Limit of Constitutional Guaranteed Time to Institute Action: 1 take the liberty to ask a question, when a person is suspected of committing a criminal offence and is actually caught hold off and taking the suspect to a court of competent jurisdiction is practically impossible alongside the fear of keeping him for more than the reasonable time as prescribed by the constitution I ask, should the suspect be allowed to go? Construing the nature and circumstances of the Nigeria criminal justice system, of course the answer should be in the negative; this is why in the words of Dr. Olu Onagoruwa,[66] holding charge is "a ploy resorted to by the police to cover their inefficiency or down right illegality by keeping arrested persons in detention beyond the constitutional limitation". Therefore, it has been strongly opined, that we should not sacrifice the fundamental right to personal liberty of

ed). And see also Toyin Doherty, Criminal Procedure in Nigeria, Blackstone press limited 1990.

[66] Annual Report 1994, A Civil Liberties Organization Report on the state of Human Right in Nigeria at p. 16.

presumably innocent citizen on the altar of crime prevention. So I ask again, should we rather sacrifice the prevention of crime (safety) for the fundamental liberty of suspect?. Construing the fact that section 14 (2) (b) of the 1999 Constitution, states that the welfare and security of the people shall be the priority government. It is observed that although we have two important model criminal processes, which are due process model and crime control model, credence should be given to the crime control model in respect of Holding charge. This is without prejudice to the due process model which proposes that crime prevention be done strictly according to law, reason being that in the society heinous crime like murder, arson, treason etc are usually carried out in remote jurisdiction by recidivist and so following due process may lead to escape and attendant freedom of suspects thereby further polluting the societal security. Applauds should be given to the Lagos state government who deemed it fit in 1979 to promulgate the Administration of justice (miscellaneous) provision Edict, amending section 236 criminal procedure law of Lagos state by adding sub-section 3 which empowers magistrate to remand after arrest. It is perhaps for this reason that I submit that a holding charge is a necessary evil buried in our legal system albeit labelled an anathema.

2. Legal Incapacity of Police to Grant Bail in some Specific Offences: the legal incapacity of the police to grant bail to criminal suspect with respect to certain offences like murder, armed robbery and treasonable colony etc. This is because the law considered these offences by their nature to be serious and they are punishable with death.

However, it should again be noted that the seriousness of an offence does not depend on the imagination of the police of office. In *Emezue v. Okola*[67] the court held that offences like attempted murder, rape, burglary, arson are serious offences. For these reason, where the police wish to detain a suspect to further investigation into the matter, without violating

---

[67] (1978) Suit No. sc 291/1976.

section 35 (5)[68] of the 1999 constitution, they have to bring him before a magistrate court for the purpose of obtaining remand order. The order if obtained will be the authority for further detention of the suspect while investigation into the case last. This practice has received judicial blessings from the words of Mukhtar JSC in *Lufadeju's case,*[69] hear him,

> The fact is that there was strong suspicion that the respondent and some others have committed an indictable offence to wit treason. After their arrest by the police there was the need to properly and lawfully keep them in custody and the only way to this was to take them to a magistrate court who would in turn remand them in custody. They couldn't possibly continue to remain in police custody without the order of a court. Police investigations some times take time, and sometimes there is the fear of a likelihood of continued committal of the same or other offences. There is the likelihood of interference with investigations, whilst this process continues or is concluded or the legal audience of the ministry of justice as sought.

3.4. The Procedures that Enabled Holding Charge

In Nigeria, two procedures have been identified as necessitating the practice of holding charge. The first to the procedure established by the observance of laws made to empower the magistrate courts or, increase the jurisdiction of the magistrate court in respect of capital offences. The second is the procedure established by practice to advert ills. We shall see them accordingly.

Procedures Established by Law

Over the years, some states in Nigeria have enacted laws with intent to increase the jurisdiction of the magistrate court, but in essence are establishing the practice of holding charge. For instance in Lagos state, there is section 236 (3) of the criminal procedure law,[70] the effect of which

---

[68] Section 35(5) shall be skeletally dealt with in this chapter.
[69] (2007) 8 NWLR (Pt. 1037) pg 535.
[70] Cap 33 Vol. 3, Laws of Lagos state, 1994 (now S. 264 of the Criminal Justice Administration Lagos State 2011, hereinafter referred to as (ACJL).

the Supreme Court held holding charge legal in the case of *Lufadeju v. Johnson.*[71]

According to section 264(1) of the criminal justice Act of Lagos State:

Any person arrested for any triable an information offence shall within a reasonable time of arrest be brought before a magistrate for remand and the magistrate shall have powers to remand such a person after examining the reasons for the arrest exhibited in the request form filed by the police, and if satisfied that there is probable cause to remand such persons, pending legal advice of the Director of public prosecution or arrangement of such person before the appropriate court or tribunal.

According to sub-section (2): where applicable, a magistrate shall grant bail to any person brought before him pursuant to sub-section (1) of this section pending the arraignment of such person before the appreciate court or tribunal.

Sub-section (10) provides thus:

In this section unless the context otherwise requires, "offence triable on information" means any offence.

a. Which on conviction shall be punished by a term of imprisonment exceeding two (2) years
b. Which on conviction shall be punished by imposition of a fine exceeding fifty thousand (₦ 50,000.00) naira; or
c. Which on conviction shall be punished by death

Also, by virtue of section 236 (3) of the criminal procedure law, trial magistrates or president of Area customary court are empowered to remand accused person in cases where they do not have jurisdiction to try the offenders. Thus, in the case of *Uwaje Nnabuife and anor v. CA. Maidoi-I. esq & anor,*[72] the court of Appeal upheld the provisions when it made the decision below.

The appeal emanated and got it roots from the proceeding in the chief magistrate court Owa-Oyibu in Delta state when the appellant were arrested at Mbiri on the 21st day of November 2004 and later charged to

---

[71] (Supra).
[72] (2007) LPELR- (A/B/262/05.

the chief magistrate court Owa-oyibu for the offence of conspiracy and armed robbery punishable under SS. 516 and 402 of the criminal code.

The magistrate decline jurisdiction to try the appellant but remanded the appellants. The appellant challenged the order made by the Chief magistrate at the High court of Justice, Owa-Oyibu, Delta state. The trial judge Osasi J. on 15th June 2005 dismissed the case of the appellant, dissatisfied with the decision of the High court, the have appealed to this court.

In conclusion, the learned justice held the appeal to be unmeritorious. The appeal was dismissed and the decision of Osasi J. delivered a 19/6/2005 was affirmed. It should be noted that the court relied heavily on the apex court decision in Lufadeju v. Johnson (supra).

Procedure Established by Practice

Apart from the power of the policies to grant bail to a suspect pending the completion of investigation under S17 or pending trail under S. 18 of CPA, it often arraigns accused persons before magistrate courts upon a holding charge. As already defined, holding charge is the practice of preferred charges especially in respect of capital offences against accused persons in magistrate courts even when such courts are obviously incompetent to try such offences. Admittedly the process of investigating crime and prosecuting offenders by the police is no doubt cumbersome and in some case the system is confronted with the problem of suspect fleeing or in some case tempering with investigation. For instance, in *Dantata v. Police*[73] the application of the accused person for bail was refused on the ground that he earlier an offered a bribe to the police in order to retrieve evidence of the offence while in police custody.

Thus, the remand procedure was introduced to ensure that accused person in deserving cases are kept in detention to enable the police conclude investigation as to whether or not such person can be arraigned. The procedure in this respect is that upon the arraignment of the accused the presiding judicial officer will order that the accused be remanded in prison custody without the plea of the accused being taken. The duration of the remand is until the arrangement of the accused person in a

[73] (1958) NNLR 3.

competent court, (contrary to this popular, the ACJA 2015 have strictly regulated the period of remand).

Apparently according to critics, this practice has been resorted to by the police to circumvent the provisions of section 35(4) of the 1999 constitution which provide to the effect that any person arrested or detained must be brought before a court of law having jurisdiction in respect of such offences within a reasonable time. Another aspect of the procedure also practiced by the police is that when the police arrest and detain a person suspected of committing a serious offence and thereafter they find themselves in serious legal problem where they do not known what to do with the accused. A prima facie evidence in support of the allegation against the suspect may be unavailable but there is hope that as the detention continues reliable evidence might be possible[74] in order to avoid actions for unlawful detention[75] or false imprisonment[76] they rush the accused to the court of law. The court is usually the magistrate court which the police know very well that it lacked jurisdiction to hear the matter. The intention of the police usually is to detain the suspect by the order of the magistrate for as long as investigation into the case last including the outcome of the DPP's advice and until there is final decision whether or not to take the case to a competent court.[77]

As rightly pointed out by Faja H,[78] the fallacy of the form of holding charge is that the accused person is only purported to be arranged, while in true fact, there is no proper arrangement. The procedure for of valid arrangement must be in conformity with section 215 of the CPA and as stated in *Lufadeju's case,*[79] wherein the Supreme Court outlined the requirement for a valid arrangement to be:

---

[74] G.O. S Amadi, Police Power in Nigeria. (Afro orbis publishing co. Ltd Nsukka 2000) pg. 198.

[75] Under section 35(6) of the constitution.

[76] False imprisonment is any detention, bodily restraint, denial of personal liberty of freedom of movement of a person in any place and in any from without lawful justification. See Ese M. Law of Tort; (Lagos, promotion publishing Co, 2008) P. 132.

[77] Dr. Okpara Okpara op cit pg. 155.

[78] Op. Cit P. 171.

[79] Supra at footnote 20.

a. The accused must be placed before the court unfiltered unless the court can see course otherwise to order.
b. The charge or information must be read over and explained to the satisfaction of the court by the register or other officer of the court.
c. It must be read and explained to him in the language he understands.
d. The accused must be called upon to plea thereto unless there exist any valid reason to do otherwise such as objection for want of service where the accused is entitled by law to service of a copy of the information and the court is satisfied that he has in fact not been duly served there with.

The court went further to say that the above stated requirement of the law are mandatory and must therefore be strictly complied in all criminal trials. While this is the law generally, the Supreme Court in same case gave leeway to the magistrates to remand person charged with criminal offences even where they lack jurisdiction to try the offence before them. There is simply a shift of the law which has received statutory blessings in our criminal justice system.[80]

3.5. Justification of Holding Charge

It is trite that two equally important model criminal processes compete for primarily in every criminal adjudication system to wit; Due process model and the crime control model. According to Igwe[81] the due process model is Supreme over the crime control model. This is because the crime control model operates within the ambit of law, that is due process model although the aim of the later (due process model) is to achieve the former (crime control model).[82] Thus, it has been opined that, no matter how involve the procedure, no matter how involved the procedure, no matter how slow the process, no matter how inconvenient the outcome, a court to

[80] We shall see these shortly.
[81] C.A. Igwe, A Legal Review of the Administration of Criminal Justice on the Magistrate Court of Ebonyi state. Ebonyi State University Law Journal (2011) vol.4 No. 1 at pg 277. op. cit p. 277.
[82] ibid.

be truly such, must insist on protecting a citizen unless and until he or she is brought within the legally defined scope of a sanction.[83]

In essence, crime control model of criminal justice administration of crime and protection of the victim rights. It has erroneously been perceived to be the bedrock or *fons et origo* of the holding charge syndrome. While this view may be correct before the judgments of the Supreme Court in *Lufadefu's case,*[84] and the promulgation of the Administration of Criminal Justice Act 2015, it is submitted that Holding charge is now predicated on the Due process model which aim is to strike a balance on the administration of criminal justice system considering the peculiarities of our policy system in Nigeria which shall be seen below.

Hence, the *abinito* crime control model basis of holding charge (now due process model basis of holding charge) was however appraised to be a sufficient reason for remand order. Due to the fact that capital offence are heinous crimes and from the vantage point of public order safety, courts at passionately to protect the society from the grievous harms of individuals with presumed high criminal propensity (the recidivist), the accused is herbal remanded for his safety and deterrence, as a warning to other (general deterrence), and for the safety of the society at large. Therefore, certain human rights must be put on hold in accordance with the law[85] for the common good of the society. Thus according to D. Peter[86] it was in the face of the increasing number of persons suspected of having committed heinous and capital offence, and the trial of whom might not commence within a reasonable time, that the Lagos state government in 1979 promulgated the Administration of Justice (miscellaneous) provisions edict.[87] This edict amended section 236 of the criminal procedure, law[88] of Lagos state by adding subsection 3 to that section. The amendment which was incorporated into the 1994 laws of Lagos state[89]

---

[83] R.A.C., Achara, Justice According to Law and Due Process: A Glance at Two of Justice Akpabio's Decisions. Unizike Law Journal Vol. 4 No.1, P. 276.

[84] Supra.

[85] See the ACJA 2015 which is not inconsistent with Human rights.

[86] Page 263 op. cit.

[87] No. 401. 1979.

[88] Cap . 32 laws of Lagos State.

[89] See Criminal Procedure Law Vol. 2 Laws of Lagos State, 1994 (Now Criminal Justice Administration, Lagos State 2011, C.JA).

provides as follows: Section 236 (3)[90] if any person arrested for any indictable offence is brought before magistrate for remand, such magistrate shall remand such person in custody or where applicable, grant him bail pending the arraignment of such person before the appropriate court for trial.

According to Fora Arthur Worrey former director of public prosecution in Lagos state,[91] the amendment became inevitable in view of the length of time it takes for the police to complete investigation into the crime and more often than not the trial delays which the frequent transfer of investigation police officers across the country counsels. Thus, it became imperative to find a legally justifiable basis for the detention of suspect, especially when the detention is beyond the limit permitted by the constitution.

It has been asserted that the nation's police force may be said to be a reflection of the society and the Nigerian police force does not appear to derogate from this assertion. Multi-tribunal problems[92] confront the Nigerian police and thwarts it's efforts to quick and successful crime investigation and prosecution. These diverse problems range from lack of personnel or adequately trained personnel, poor remuneration and lack of requisite equipment and infrastructure to engender motivation, commitment and efficiency. The combination of all these result in a situation of nonchalance, and lackadaisical attitude on the part of the police to crime investigation. Hence, the resort to filling of the holding charge in a court lacking jurisdiction and the resultant gross violation of human rights of the person concerned.[93]

Even when the case file is eventually sent to the appropriate department of the ministry of justice for legal advice if sometimes merely marks another phase of delayed justice for the accused person. The cause

---

[90] Now section 264 (1) of the C. J.A.

[91] Cited in D. Peter Op. cit P. 264.

[92] Akinyede, GBA "The Barr, the police and the judiciary" (1958) Nigeria Law, journal Vol. 1, No.2 and see also O. Ohonbamu. The Delimina of police organization: under a federal system: The Nigerian example (1972) Nigerian Law Journal Vol.6. No.1 Johnson Adeyemi, "Nigerian police, the limit of oppression" the legal practitioners review Vol.1.

[93] D. Peter Op. Cit 257.

of delay here is not uncommonly associated with under staffed[94] but are also cash strapped. Thus apart from inadequate personnel, mundane things required to keep an office functioning such as files etc are sometimes not available. This eventually results in unnecessary delay in the issuance of legal advice by the professional staff of the ministries and when a decision is finally taken to prosecute the actual filling of information in the High court or at the appropriate tribunal may yet take a much longer period. In all cases, the accused right is being violated, this is the reason why Holding charge has now been strictly given bounds and regulations by the law and the supreme court, the due process of holding charge now, is first to safe the criminal justice system and second, to ensure that upon it instrumentality, its fundamental right is being violated.

3.6. Holding Charge *vis-a-vis* the Administration of Criminal Justice Act 2015 and the 1999 Constitution as Amended

This part of the discourse is the most important and crucial towards establishing the fact that holding charge is legal and thus a necessary evil in our legal system. The discourse shall proceed with a direct deliberation and dilation of the subject matter. In the face of the 1999 constitution as amended and the Administration of Criminal Justice Act 2015, while receiving scholarly and judicial blessings from the courts and jurist alike.

For purposes of scholarship, I shall proceed by interrogating some sections of the constitution, section 36 (1) of the constitution (as amended) provides as follows: in the determination of his civil rights and obligations including any question or determination by or against any government as authority a person shall be entitled to a fair hearing within a reasonable time by a court or other tribunal established by laws and constituted in such a manner as to secure its independence and impartiality. The legal implication of the above section is that every person or authority has a

---

[94] The salaries and general conditions of service of state Attorneys are not encouraging enough to attract legal practitioners to accept appointment in the ministries of justice. For instance; Lawyere in Ogun state ministry of justice had to embark on strike action to press for increased salaries and exchanges remunerated. See the guardian newspaper. Tuesday June 3rd, 1997, P.3.

right to fair hearing when it comes to the determination of his civil rights and obligations.[95]

According section 36(5) states that "every person who is charged with a criminal offence shall be presumed to be innocent until he is proved guilty. The proviso state that nothing in this section shall invalidate any law by reason only that the law imposes upon any such person the burden to proving particular facts.

The legal implication of this section is strictly the presumptions of innocent of a person charges with a criminal offence, although without prejudice to any law policy evidential burden on the person.[96] Also, every person who is charged with a criminal offence shall be entitled, to be informed promptly in the language that he understands and in detail the nature of the offence, be given adequate time and facilities for the preparation of his defence, and to defend himself in person or by legal practitioner of his own choice.[97]

However, having blazed the trail guiding the trial of both civil and criminal litigation, section 35 guarantees the liberty of every person and makes provision for some salient areas dealing directly with this research work. For purposes of clarity it purpose to reproduce and dilate on this provisions accordingly:

Section 35(1) states; Every person shall be entitled to his personal liberty and no person shall be deprived of such liberty save in the following cases and in accordance with a procedure permitted by law, and paragraph C provides for the purpose of bringing him before a court in execution of the order of a court but or upon reasonable suspicion of his having committed a criminal offence, or to such extent as may be reasonably necessary to prevent his committing a criminal offence.

The practical implication of this section is that, whereas every person has a right to liberty, but this right is qualified, and the main focus on our discourse is provided for in sub 1 paragraph c of that same section for

---

[95] See *Adigun v. A.g Oyo state* (1997) 1 NWLR pt 53. P 678 SC per Nna-Emeka Agu, *FCSC v. Laoye* (1989) 2 NWLR pt. 106.p 265 at 681, *Local Government Board v. Atliga* (1915) AC 120. *Oyeyemi v. Commissioner for Local Government kwara* (1993) 6 NWLR pt 229. P 344 Sc, *LDPC v. Fawehimmi* 1985 2 NWLR pt. 7. p 3000 at 270 Supreme court.
[96] Ibid.
[97] Section 36(6) 1999 constitution.

purposes of brining a person to court for committing or suspected to have committed an offence.[98] In the same vein, sub section (4) of that same section provides that, any person who is arrested or detained in accordance with section shall be brought before a court of law within a reasonable time, and if he is not tried him a period of:

a. Two months from the date of his arrest or detention in the case of a person who is in custody or is not entitled to bail; or
b. Three months from the date of his arrest or detention in the case of a person who has been released on bail.

The section continues by rounding up that, he shall (without prejudice to any further proceedings that may be brought against him) be released either unconditionally or upon such conditions as are reasonably necessary to ensure that he appears for trail at a later date. It should be parenthetically noted that the import of this sections is that, any persons arrested or detained shall be brought to a court within a reasonable time for purpose of trial, and if he is not tried within two months for persons entitle to bail or within three months for persons released on bail, he shall be relieved of the process either constitutionally or unconditionally to ensure his due appearance on a later date. It should be parenthetically noted that the import of the sections is that, any person arrested or detained shall be brought to a court within a reasonable time, for purposes of trial, and he is not tried within two month persons not entitle to bail or within three months person released on bail he shall be released of the process either conditionally or unconditionally to ensure his due appearance on a later date.[99]

Interestingly, the expression, a reasonable time mentioned in sub section (4) of the foregoing section is defined in sub-section 5. For purpose of clarity, section 35 (5) states that, "In sub-section (4) of this section, the expression "a reasonable time" means:

---

[98] See *Hussein v. kam* (1964) 3 All Er 1626. *Agbale v COP* (1969) 1 NMLR 137 hc 1968 1 NWLR 176 CA, *Walter v. Smith and songs limited* (194) 1 KB 595.
[99] *Bamaiyi v the State* (2001) 8 NWLR pt 7 15, P272 SC *Likita v Cop* (2002) 11 NWLR pt 777 pt 145 CA, see Anaekwe cop (supra).

a. In the case of an arrest or detention in any place where there is a court of competent jurisdiction within a radius of forty kilometer, a period of one day; and
b. In any other case, a period as in the circumstance may be considered by the court to be reasonable.[100]

It should be parenthetically noted that a reasonable time means 1 to 2 day or such longer period as in the circumstances maybe considered by the court to be reasonable, it therefore means that the court may decide a reasonable time to be after two days or such other time. The meaning of reasonable in this regards is circumstantial and depends on the court.

Consequentially, it is expedient at this juncture to introduce the relevant provision of the administration of Criminal Justice Act 2015. However before a cursory look at that, it is necessary to note down the following preliminary points. First, contrary to old popular views, holding charge and remand has now gained legality in federal and state statutes. Second, the provisions of the ACJA 2015 specifically section 293-299 are not contrary to section 35 and 36 of the constitution but rather complementary. Third, the time and process for a Holding charge is *in tandem* with section 35 (4) (5) of the constitution. Fourth, the discordant tunes about holding charge is due to insufficient appreciation of the law. Therefore part 30 of the ACJA 2015 which provides for detention time limits provides in section 293 (1) that "A suspect arrested for an offence which a magistrate court has no jurisdiction to try shall within a reasonable time of arrest, be brought before a magistrate court for remand.

Sub (2) states that, "An application for remand under this section shall be made *ex parte* and shall:

a. be made in the prescribed "Report and Request for Remand form" as contained in form 8, in the first schedule to this Act; and
b. be verified on oath and contain reasons for the remand request

Section 294 (1) provides further that; where the court after examining the reason for the arrest and for the request for remand in accordance with

---

[100] See with approval the following authorities- *Bamayi v. the State* (Supra), *Murphy v. DPP* (1990) 2 All Er 390.

the provisions of section 293 of the Act, is satisfied that there is probable cause to remand the suspect pending the receipt of a copy of the legal advice from the Attorney- General of the Federation and arrangement of the suspect before the appropriate court, as the case maybe, may remand the suspect in custody.

Sub (2) of the same sections provides that; in considering whether "probable cause" has been established for the remand of a suspect pursuant to subsection (1) of this section, the court may take into consideration of the following:

a. The nature and seriousness of the alleged offence
b. Reasonable grounds for believing that the suspect may abscond or commit further offence where he is not committed to custody; and
c. Reasonable grounds to suspect that the suspect has been involved in the commission of the alleged offence.
d. Any other circumstance of the case that justifies the request for remand.

While section 293 provides for the actual authority conferred on the magistrate court for remand of suspects in prison custody, section 294 particularly sub (2) describes a probable cause for the grant of this order spanning from paragraph A to C of the sub section, these without doubts and much emphasizes represents the jurisprudence behind the granting of the order.

One of the obvious feature of this section is that the order for remand would always be made after the magistrate discovers what is a probable cause, depending on the facts and circumstances of a particular case. What is probable cause is objective and may be ascertained factually. It is the duty of the prosecution (in this case the police) to show probable cause, that would warrant remand. Happily, subsection (2) of section 294 provides for virtues to guide the trial magistrate in search of whether there is a probable cause.

At this juncture, the provision of 35 (1) (c) is relevant which provides that, a persons may be deprived of his liberty only in accordance with produce permitted by law for purpose of bringing the suspect before of court of law upon reasonable suspicion of his committing an offence or to such extent as maybe reasonably necessary to prevent his committing an offence. It is trite that this provision pertains only to appearance before a court of a suspect upon reasonable suspicion. Some jurist like Ibrahim Abdullahi[101] has submitted that the combine provision of section 36 and 35, "the position seems to be in Nigeria, no person should be taken to court unless the charge against him on first information report as settled and the prosecuting authorities are prepared to go on with the trial against him. Under section 36(1) of the 1999 constitution, a person shall be entitled to a fair hearing within a reasonable time. It is therefore argued that criminal cases when taken to court should be ripe for hearing not for either further investigations and that suspects and or accused persons are not there on mere suspicion which cannot be regarded as reasonable suspicion as required under section 35 (1) (c) of the 1999 constitution".[102]

However, contrary to the above position it is submitted that the discovery probable course in section 293 and 294 in the ACJA 2015 pertains only to a remand proceeding and not a full flesh trial. The drafters of the ACJA should be applauded for the test of probable cause.

More germane to our discourse is the provision of the 1999 constitution alongside the ACJA 2015 as pertaining to time and protocol in order not to violate pre trial rights under the fundamental human rights.[103] Before the trail is blazed some preliminary points need be noted for purposes of clarity. First, that the provision of section 35 of the constitution and section 293-299 of the ACJA 2015 shown no inconsistency. Second, while the constitution 35 (5) defines a reasonable time and applies to the maximum period a person arrested or detained at a police station should be brought before the court for remand, section 293 (1) of the ACJA 2015 only provides that a person arrested for an offence must be brought to court within a reasonable time of arrest without stating hours or numbers of days. However, reasonable time has already been

---

[101] I. Abdullahi (FRHD) LLB, BL, LLM, PHD in view. The Supreme court of Nigeria decision in *Lufadeju v Johnson case* 2007 8 WNR pt 1037 pg 535- whether unconstitutionality of holding charge in Nigeria? Journal of law, policy and globalization vol. 29, 2014 at pg. 90.

[102] Ibid at 91. He cited with approval *Suleman v. COP Plateau State* (2003) 21 WRN per Niki Tobi JSC.

[103] See section 33, 34 and 35 1999 constitution.

defined by the constitution as 1 to 2 days or any such time as court may consider. There is nothing in sections 293-299 of ACJA 2015 contradicting the provisions of section 35 (4) (5) of the constitution.

As it was stated above, the discourse shall be focused on time limit in both instruments. Section 296 sub (1) of the ACJA 2015 provides that, "Where an order of remand of the suspect is made pursuant to section 293 of this Act, the order shall be for a period not exceeding 14 days in the first instance, and the case shall be returnable within the same period".

Sub (2) states thus, "where on application in writing good cause is shown why there should be an extension of the remand period, the court may make an order for further remand of the suspect for a period not exceeding 14 days and make the proceedings returnable within, the same period. Sub (4) further states; at the expiration of the remanded with his trial having not been filed at the relevant court having jurisdiction, the court shall issue a hearing notice on:

a. The inspector General of police and Attorney General of the Federation
b. The commissioner of Police of the State of the Federal Capital Territory or the Attorney-General of the federation, as the case maybe or
c. Only relevant authority in whose custody the suspect is or at whose instance the suspect is remanded and adjourn the matter within a period not exceeding 14 days of the expiration of the period of remand order made under subsection (1) or (2) of this section, to inquire as to the position of the case and for the inspector General of police and the Attorney-General of the federation to show cause why the suspect remanded should not be unconditionally released.

The forgoing section is clear and limits remand order to a period of 14 day at the first I instance and another 14 days upon renewal by showing good cause for extension of remand order. Further, the Act gives the court the right to issue hearing justice on the inspector General of police and Attorney-General of the federation or any other authority to show cause why the suspect should not released unconditionally. It is only where, they show cause as provided in sub-section (4) that sub section 5 (a and b)[104] empowers the court to further make an extension of the remand of the suspect for a final period not exceeding 14 day. But where no good cause is shown, subsection (16) empowers the court with or without application to effect the discharge of the suspect immediately from custody. This sub-section portrays how delight and strict the Act strives to make pre-trial rights sacrosanct and sacred. Sub section 7 states emphatically that, no further application for remand shall be entertained by any court after the proceeding in subsection (6) of this section.

Prof Fagbohun,[105] shares the view that at this stage, it has to be remembered that, the view that section 35 (5) of the constitution applies to the maximum period a person arrested or detained at a police station should be brought before a court for remand"

The learned Professor went onto say, "Section 35 (4) of the constitution, which provides for a period of two months or three months as the case maybe after which a person arrested or remanded maybe released by the court conditionally or unconditionally to ensure he appears for trial at a later date, on the other hand, the maximum period a person in remand awaiting trial is expected to stay under sections 293-299 of the ACJA 2015 before the court will discharge him in the event that the advice of the Attorney-General is not forthcoming is the overall period of 42 days- split into first 14 days, second 14 days and third 14 days. This is obvious under section 35 (5) of the constitution which permit up to 2 or 3 months. So it should be noted hence, that the right to liberty guaranteed in section 35 is limited amongst others under subsection is provided for in subsection (4) to mean a maximum period of 2 or 3 months as the case may be and the ACJA 2015 is in line with these provisions. The case of *Mrs. E. A Lufadeju (Chief magistrate grade 1) and Attorney-General of Lagos state v. Evangelist Bayo Johnson*[106] is instructive at this point.

Evangelist Bayo Johnson (the respondent) was arrested on the 12th of January 1997 for conspiracy to commit treason and the commission of treasonable felony. He was taken along with eleven (11) others before

---

[104] ACJA 2015.
[105] Ibid.
[106] (2007) 8 NWLR (pt 1037).

Grade 1 on the 12th of March 1999 of Lagos. The charges were read but the plea of the accused person was not taken. An oral application for bail was made on the same day, Mrs. E. A. Lufadeju (1st Appellant) refused the application on the ground that she lacks powers to entertain and consider a bail application in respect of a capital offence such as treason. The Respondent and others were remanded in custody at the force C. I. D Alagbon, Lagos. The plea of evangelist Bayo Johnson was not taken although the charges were read to him as a result of the refusal of bail and remand in prison custody of the respondent, he filed an action at the High Court by way of an application under the fundamental Right (Enforcement procedure) roles. He asked for a declaration that his detention prompted by the magistrate order was unconstitutional and urged the court to quash the order. He also claimed N5,000:000,00 (Five million Naira only) as damages for his illegal detention. The High Court dismissed, the application it declared that the magistrate order of 12th March 1997 was a valid order and that the proceedings of that day was a remand proceedings under section 236 (3) of the criminal procedure law of Lagos state.

Evangelist Bayo Johnson was dissatisfied with the decision of the High Court and appealed to the Court of Appeal which allowed the appeal. The court held that section 236 (3) of the Criminal Procedure Laws of Lagos State conflicts with the constitution. Both the orders of the magistrate and that of the High Court were set aside. Mr. E. A. Lafadeju and her co-appellants were dissatisfied with the judgment and the appealed to the Supreme Court of Nigeria. The Argument of the Appellants in the main was that, the proceedings before the magistrate were remand proceedings and not arraignment. The respondent contended the opposite.

The Supreme Court of Nigeria considered sections 78 (b), 215, 118 (11) and 236 (3) of the Criminal Procedure Law of Lagos State 1994, sections, 32 (1) (c), 33 (4), 33 (5) and (6) of the 1979 constitution, section 35 of the Criminal Code,[107] section 215 Criminal Procedure Law,[108] Articles 7 (1) (b) and (d) of the African charter on Human and peoples right 1979 as well as order 1 Rule 2(b) and (3) of the fundamental Rights

---

[107] (supra).

[108] Cap 30, Vol.2, Laws of Lagos State of Nigeria 1994.

(Enforcement procedures Rule) 1979[109] and at page 53 paragraph A-B of the report where the case was reported,[110] the Supreme Court validated the incarceration of Evangelist Bayo Johnson without trial in the following wordings;

" ...Section 236 (3) of the Criminal Procedure Law is not unconstitutional. Rather, it clearly complements the provisions of section 32 of the 1979 constitution and is designed to aid administration of criminal justice in the country...."

Similarly at page 573 paragraph B-C, the Supreme Court held as follows:

> ... The Court owes it a duty not to pay with allegation as grave as treasonable felony. Neither individual liberty and freedom. Therefore, what section 236 (3) of the Criminal Procedure Law does is to maintain a balance between the two by doing away with the tendency of arbitrary indefinite police detention of suspect without order of court...

In this case, WSN Onnoghen, JSC (and subsequently CJN as he then was) at page 40 para E-G in dealing with the question as to whether a magistrate has power of remand even where he lacks jurisdiction over the matter? His Lordship said, "A Magistrate to have jurisdiction to act these under, the persons to be remanded or possibly granted bail where the court has the jurisdiction to so grant, must have been arrested for indictable offence such as treasonable felony which is outside the competence or jurisdiction of the magistrate to try. In such a situation the magistrate to try. In such a situation the magistrate is empowered, upon the suspect being brought before him, to remand the suspect in custody pending the arrangement of such person before a court of competent jurisdiction to toy the said indictable offence. Although it has been stated or plethora of diction in the court of trail goes to the root of the matter so as to sustain a nullity the trial judges decision in respect of the relevant subject, the extent position of the law as stated in *Lufadeju's case* is the Law and may serve as a special exception in cases of remand proceedings. It should be taken note at the juncture that the criminal procedure of Lagos should be

[109] Cap 49, laws of former Bendel state of Nigeria 1976.

[110] Now amended as the fundamental Rights Enforcement procedure rules) 2009.

applauded, and have gained judicial flavor since 2007, so the provisions of the ACJA as regards detention is not new. This is due to the fact that they share in spirit and letters and intent the same provision. Accordingly, no withstanding the widespread criticisms of Holding Charge, it is valid and must be obeyed till set aside[111] by virtue of the doctrine of judicial precedents.

Thus in *UBA. Trustees Ltd v. Niger Ceramic,*[112] Nna-Emeka Agu JSC (as he then was) said:

> In our hierarchical system of court, the law is in the final analysis of what the Supreme Court says it is once they have decided a point of law their decision as the doctrine of stare decision is biding on all other courts in the country. The farthest to which any court can go is to criticize but apply.

In *Odi v. Osafile,*[113] Obaseki JSC (of blessed memories) said, "...Laws are made for men and not men for laws..." it should however be noted that the Criminal procedure code law[114] and penal code have no equivalent provision of section 236 (3) in the Lagos states law that recognized remand proceedings. The practice under the Criminal Procedure Code is that the police should take a person to court after being satisfied that on the fact at their disposal, a prima, facie case can be established on the charge against such a person.

So to this extent, the right of the accused person is no way violated. Therefore, the present tenor of the law should be followed accordingly, and it should be noted that the law is made for the society and not the society for the law. The practice of Holding charge is constitutional and statutory.

---

[111] (2007)8 NWLR (pt 1037) p. 535.

[112] Like *Obikoya v. Registrar of Companies*(1975) 4 S.C at 34 22 NSCQR (pt. 11) 574 at p. 592: Alliance of Democracy v *Peter Ayadele Fayose & 4 ors* (2005) 10 NWLR (pt 1932) 151 p.188.

[113] (1987) 3 NWLR (pt 62) Act 23.

Chapter Four

The Rights of Suspects and the Effects of Holding Charge

4.1. Introduction

Human rights, as we know them today, assumed formidable dimensions in the post world war II years, capitalized by the desire of people and nations to redefine, reassert and restore the intrinsic worth and dignity of man after the bitter ravages and savagery of that war. The desire found expression in concrete terms on December 10, 1948 when the General Assembly of the United Nations Organization (UNO) adopted the Universal Declaration of Human Rights.

However, the philosophical foundations of human rights are traceable to the Natural law theories of the early times.[115] In that view, nature endowed man with certain rights which protect and preserve the sacredness of the human person as inviolable, equal to the fellow man, free and independent. The Natural law Theory emphasizes the universal nature of the right of man. As Naill MacDermott puts it human are part of the common heritage of all mankind without discrimination on grounds of rally sex, religious or other differences. These rights, common to all mankind, have along history many of them finding their origin in religions teachings. But now, in our lifetime, they have been formulated more fully than ever before and agreed to by all peoples from all parts of the world.[116]

---

[115] Osita Eze: Human Rights in Africa: some selected problems. (Nigeria Institute of International Affairs, Lagos, in co-operation with Macmillan Nigeria publishers limited, 1984) Ashield Samony: Human Rights as international consensus: the making of the Universal Declaration of Human Rights (thesis for the candidate of Philosophy, Department of History University of Bergen; May 1990).

[116] Nail MacDermott: Opening Address to the International Conference on Human Rights Education in rural Environments, Lagos, Nigeria, 1985. P. 10. For other contributions

Nigeria's fundamental human rights provision[117] are essentially civil and political in nature apparently on the recommendation of the Willinks Commission Report on minorities.[118] The other categories of rights are represented under the fundamental objectives and directive principles of state policies[119] which are however non justiciable.[120]

Unfortunately, many a jurist and scholars has fallen into the error and misconceptions of understanding the relationship and effects of holding charge on the Fundamental Human Rights of suspects. The chapter will analyze the Fundamental Human Rights and answer the question as to whether or not those rights have been violated.

4.2. The Meaning of Human Rights

The concept of human rights, like most juristic concepts, evades an apt definition. According to Prof. Nwazuoke,[121] one point of major agreement is that the addition of the effective human to rights indicate that the rights in question belong solely to human being, and that all is needed to have them is human nature. It is on this basis that they have been described as inalienable.[122] In 1945, the nations of the world realized and expressed in the charter of the United Nations,[123] that the future peace of the world, depended on the guaranteeing to every man, woman and child of certain fundamental human rights and freedoms. In a succession of declarations and charters since then, on almost every continent upon the

---

along this line, see chukwudifu Oputa. Human rights in political and legal culture of Nigeria, at the second Idigbe memorial lectures 1986, P. 45 Chukwuweike Idigbe. Fundamental Rights provisions of the constitution at all Nigerian judges Conference papers, 1982 (London, sweet and Maxwell, 1983). P.47. *ransom Kuti V Attorney General of the Federation* (1985) 2 NWLR (pt 6) 211., M. Granston, "Human Rights Today," reported from A.J. Mitre: should we have a Bill Rights?" (1997) 40 MLR 389 at 392.

[117] Chapter iv of the 1999 constitution (as amended) (hereinafter referred to as the constitution).

[118] A. Ojo Fundamental Human Right in Nigeria; The 1963 and 1979 constitutional provisions, Nigerian journal of contemporary law (1977-1980); p.118.

[119] Chapter 2 of the 1999 constitution as amended.

[120] By virtue of section 6(6) (c) of the 1999 constitution.

[121] A.N Nwazuoke, Introduction to Human Rights Law (Abakaliki, copy craft in't Ltd, 2006) P.7.

[122] Ibid.

[123] The League of Nations was the precursor of the United Nations Organization.

globe, those rights end freedom have been enshrined as among the most precious aspirations of the people.

Human rights include but are not limited to these civil and political rights, which are recognized and protected in the domestic constitutional jurisprudence of most modern nations.[124] Civil and political rights are essentially conceptualized as checks on the abuse of state power, and include to rights to privacy, free movement, personal liberty, free association, equality before the law etc.

Human rights have been described by the naturalist school of jurisprudence as inalienable and proceeding from the law of nature and not as a gift of any civil authority.[125] The philosophical foundations of human rights are traceable to the natural law theories of the early times. There are rights that are created by nature, it's a gift of nature protected by the constitution. Chapter 2 and 4 of the constitution guarantees them.[126] Prof Osita Eze defined human rights as; Demands or claims which individual or groups make on a society, some of which are protected by law and have become part of the *Lexlata* , while others remain aspiration to be attained in the future.[127] The apex court had also defined it in the case of *Ransome Kuti v. A. G. federation*[128] Per kayode Eso JSC (as he then was) when he said that human rights; is a right which stands above the ordinary laws of the land and which is in part antecedent to the political society itself. It is a primary condition to a civilized existence and what has been by our constitution since independent is to have these rights enshrined in the constitution that the right could be immutable to the extent of the non-immutability of the constitution itself.

Fundamental rights derived from the natural or fundamental law. In *Igwe V. Ezean Ochie,*[129] it was held to be universal in the sense that all people have and should enjoy them and to be independent in the sense that the exist and are available as standards of justification and criticism

---

[124] See chapter IV of the Constitution.

[125] Thomas Jefferson, cited J. Steimer and Philip Alston (2000) international Human Right in context 2nd edition, Oxford. P. 325.

[126] Chapter 2 is non-justiciable.

[127] Osita Eze, Human Right in Africa: selected problems (Lagos: Macmillan, 1984) P.5.

[128] (1985) 2 NWLR (pt.6) 211 at 230.

[129] (2010) 7 NWLR (pt 1192).

whether or not they are recognized and implemented by the legal system or official of a country. The moral doctrine of fundamental right aims at identifying the fundamental prerequisites for each human being leading a minimally good life. The fundamental right law in Nigeria is contained inter-alia in two major documents. These are the 1999 constitution of the Federal Republic of Nigeria and the African charter on Human and peoples' rights (Ratification and Enforcement) Act.[130]

The statute book gave protection to those rights written in there and also provide for due enforcement. Thus if a person fell that his or her rights have been breached or contravened by any person or authority, such person is allowed to apply in the high court of the state for redress.[131]

However, the improper use of remand proceedings on Holding charge may sometime result to violation of some Fundamental Human Right but let it be remembered that, the fact that Holding charge is constitutional having been realized, this chapter deals with the questions on whether or not Holding charge violate fundamental human rights. It must however be acknowledged that the improper administration of the law as regards holding charge may result to violation of any of the rights but basically no violation is recorded. But when the violation is occurs a particular set of persons (prisoners) are relied upon to support the outcome, that is the Awaiting Trial Person (ATP). This category of persons bears the outcome of the improper use of Holding charge.

4.3. The Right to Personal Liberty

The right to personal liberty is perhaps one of the most cherished of all right, probably next in importance to the right of life. Professor Stone has well written that:

> "One of the hallmarks of a free society is the ability of its citizen to go about their businesses without the need to anyone in authority, what they are doing and without the fear that they maybe subject to arbitrary challenge or arrest".[132]

---

[130] Cap. A.9 LFN 2004.

[131] See Section.46(1) & (2) of the constitution.

[132] Prof. Richard Stone, Textbook on Civil liberties, Blackstone Press Ltd, London, 1994, P.29.

According to Dr. Okpara Okpara,[133] every person no matter his or her condition in life views his liberty or physical freedom as a priceless attribute as a humans being created in the image of God himself with rational possibilities. Lord Denning in a general sense defined right to personal liberty as, the freedom of every law abiding citizens to think what he will, to say what he will on the lawful occasions without let or hindrance from any other person.[134]

The above statement must not be seen as entirely descriptive of personal liberty as it appear not to recognize the limitations on individual rights to personal liberty. The following comments of Justice Pius Aderemi[135] attempts to achieve the balance required in formulating an acceptable definition of the right to personal liberty.

From the above, therefore right to personal liberty is the right not to be subjected to imprisonment, arrest and any other physical coercion in any manner that does not admit of legal justification.[136]

In *Liverside v. Anderson,*[137] Lord Atkin said that, in English law every imprisonment is prima facie unlawful and that it is for a person directly imprisonment to justify his act.

The right to personal liberty is prescribed under section 35 (1) of the constitution as follows:

1. Every person shall be entitled to his personal liberty and no person shall be deprived of such liberty save in the following cases and in accordance with a procedure permitted by law;
   a. In execution of the sentence or order of a court in respect of a criminal offence of which he has been found guilty.
   b. Reason of his failure to comply with the order of a court or in order to secure the fulfillment of any obligation imposed upon him by law
   c. For the purpose of bringing him before a court in execution of the order of a court or upon reasonable suspicion of his having

[133] Dr. Okpara, Okpara op. cit p.139.
[134] Lord Denning, Freedom under the Law (1949) P.5.
[135] *Eyu v. State*(1988) 2 NWLR (pt. 78) 602-626.
[136] E.C.S Wade, Law of the Constitution, 10ed; chap. 5, pp. 207-208.
[137] (1942) A.C 206.

committed a criminal offence, or such extent as maybe reasonably necessary to prevent his community a criminal offence.

d. In the case of persons suffering from infections or contagious disease, person's of unsound mind, persons addicted to drugs or alcohol or vagrants for the purpose of their case or treatment or the protection of the community

e. For the purposes of preventing the unlawful entry of any person into Nigeria of effecting the expulsion, extradition or other lawful removal from Nigeria of any person or the taking of proceedings relating there to;

Provided that a person who is charged with an offence and who has been detained in lawful custody awaiting trial shall not continue to be kept in such detention for a period longer than the maximum period of imprisonment prescribed for the offence.

Similarly Article 6 to the African charter on human and people's rights[138] provides that;

Every individual shall have the right to liberty and to the security of his person. No one may be deprived his freedom except for reasons and conditions previously laid down by law. In particular no one may be arbitrary arrested or detained. Subsumed in the personal liberty are other rights of a custodial detainee, these includes the right not be in a custody awaiting trial for longer period than the maximum period of imprisonment prescribed for the offence[139] right to silence[140] right to be arraigned within a reasonable.[141] The issue abound when it is noted that a person detained must be brought before a court of law within a reasonable time.

---

[138] (Ratification and enforcement) Act Cap. LFN 2004. The African charter is part of the laws of Nigeria and therefore should be accorded equal weight with it regard being had to international obligations Nigeria has assumed under the charter. See *Oguju v. State* (1994) 9 NWLR (pt 366) *Abacha v. Fewehinm.*(Supra).

[139] This is perhaps, the most observable lapse in holding charge phenomenon suspects are kept awaiting trial for periods much longer than they would have remained in prison custody if they were convicted for the alleged offences.

[140] This is the presumption against self incrimination that is constitutionally recognized under section 36(1) of the co.

[141] Section 36(4) of the constitution, prescribes two months of persons under custodial arrest and three months for other cases. In other words no person shall be in detention without arrangement for layer than three months.

It has been argued bluntly that persons detained under holding charge are held for the purpose of being brought before courts in execution of court order.

Recall that in *Bayo Johnson v Lufadeju*[142] one of the issue raised for determination by the supreme was whether the court of appeal was right to hold that section 236(3) CPL of Lagos state was in direct conflict with section 32 of the 1979 constitution (now section 35 1999 constitution) and other relevant provision.

WSN Onnoghen JSC (as he then was) holds the view that section 236(3) of the CPL is not unconstitutional and that the lower courts was in error when it held that it is if anything, the said section clearly complements the provisions of section 32 of the 1979 constitution and is designed to aid the administration of criminal justice in the country".

My Lord, Akinta JSC was pungent, thus " it is necessary to state that section 263 (3) CPL is aimed at ensuring judicial control of those arrested by the police on criminal allegations". He went further thus; the procedure is totally burned by the provisions of section 32(1)C of the 1979 constitution because what was done at that stage was that the court ordered that the respondent be remanded in custody upon an allegation by the police that he (respondent) was on reasonable suspicion of having committed treasonable offence and actually committing treasonable offence".

His Lordship Niki Tobi JSC was more thoughtful, thus, "the purpose of section 236 (3) CPL is to provide for the remand of persons while preparation for arrangement continuous, it is actually an intermediate stage between arrest and the institution of criminal proceeding".

It is submitted that the provisions of section 236(3) CPL as well as 293-299 of the ACJA 2015 and other state domesticated laws has received judicial blessings as constitutional and complementary of the right to liberty.

[142] Supra.

4.4. The Right to Fair Trial within Reasonable Time

Not withstanding the glittering provisions of Nigerian law on the speedy administration of criminal justice in Nigeria, the reality is that the law is honoured more in the breach than in the observance. The chorus 'justice delayed is justice denied has become a senseless nuisance to most of the persons and institutions which are ultimately connected with the administration of justice in our country and a totally bankrupt system of administration of justice. This is of course extremely, since that chorus is absolutely true.[143]

Section 36(4) of the constitution provides: whenever any person is charged with a criminal offence, he shall, unless the charged is withdrawn be entitled to a fair hearing in public within a reasonable time by a court or tribunal, provided that;

a. A court or such a tribunal may exclude from its proceeding persons other than the parties that or their legal practitioner in the interest of defence, public safety, public morality, the welfare of persons who have not attained the age of eighteen years, the protection of the private lives of the parties or for such extent as it may consider necessary by reason of special circumstances in which publicity would be contrary to the interests of justice.
b. If any proceedings before a court or such tribunal, a minister of the government of the federation or a commissioner of the government of a state satisfies the court or tribunal that it would not be in the public interest for any matter to be publicly disclosed, the court or tribunal shall make arrangements for evidence relating to that matter to be heard in private and shall take such other actions as may be necessary or expedient to prevent the disclosure of the matter.

Similarly, Article 7 (1) (d) of the African charter provides that, Every individual shall have his cause heard comprises: they right to be tried within a reasonable time by an impartial court or tribunal.

[143] T.A. Aguda : The challenge for Nigeria Law and Nigeria Lawyers in the 21st century "a Nigerian National Merit Award Winners lecturer, presented on September 14,1938 at 3-4.

The above provisions as well as Article 10 of the United Nations Universal Declaration on Human Right[144] (UDHR) guarantee fair trial; it provides thus; Everyone is entitled in full equality to a fair and public hearing by an independent and impartial tribunal in the determination of his rights and obligations and of any criminal charge against him.

The right to fair trial within a reasonable time[145] embodies two important components namely, the right to fair hearing and the right to speedy trial. It is imperative to note that two components differ fundamentally. While trial is all encompassing, that is from arrangement to the conclusion of the trial intimating in the announcing of the decision of the court or tribunal, fair hearing entails merely from arrangement to the putting of the case for the defence.[146]

The logical conclusion garnered from the statement above is that fair hearing only accrues or comes to play only if a full arraignment of the accused takes place.[147] I take total exception to that position with due respect. Fair hearing is a matter that must be given full ascription a judicial or main judicial process.

Accordingly, contrary to the view that Holding charge is in conflict with right of an accused to fair trial within a reasonable time, it is submitted that there is no conflict. In *Bayo Johnson's case*[148] His Lordship Aloma Marian Mukhtar JSC delivering the lead judgment said, after observing that learned counsel to the respondent in his submissions stated that section 263 (3) CPL was in conflict with section 33 (4) of the 1979 constitution (now 36(4) of the 1999 constitution), held that " what is

---

[144] (1948) General Assembly Resolution 274 (111).

[145] Reasonable Time is the shortest time a cause or matter ought to be heard and determined having regard to the dictates of the law and requirement of fair hearings. Beyond the said period, inordinate delay, which vitiate fair hearing sets in. See A. O. Obaseki (justice) . "Defeating Delay-case flow management; A keynotw Address delivered at a seminar for legal practitioners organized by Continuing Legal Education Association of Nigeria (CLAN) in lagos, Nigeria on March 16, 1994 at P.3.

[146] A. A. Adeyemi, Criminal Justice Administration in Nigeria in the context of the African charter on Human and people Rights: in Kahi, A and Osibands(eds) (1992) perspectives on Human Right. Pp. 121-141 at 129.

[147] Because the following provisions are perceived to be absent: section 36(6) (a,b,c and d).

[148] (2007) 8 NWLR (Pt 1037) p. 535.

responsible time is subjective and since this is dependent on the completion of investigations; all factors will be taken into consideration.

My Lord disagreed with the submissions of counsel that section 263 (3) CPL is in conflict with in section 33 (4) of the 1979 constitution.

The prevalent misconception about this specific right is that, it is the popular view that, persons detained under a holding charge are not given the opportunity to take his plea before the remand order, therefore the right to fair hearing is being breached. It is however contended in this research that the nature of a holding charge is ex parte[149] and it applies only to capital offence still within the constitutionally provided time to commence full trial. So no violation of fair hearing is occasioned.

4.5. The Right to Presumption of Innocence

A rebuttable presumption of law refers to the inference drawn from specific facts, which are conclusive until disproved by evidence to the contrary.[150]

The concept of presumption of innocence is a rebuttable presumption of law. Presumption of innocence is exemplified in section 36 (5) of the constitution, as follows: Every person who is charged with a criminal offence shall be presumed to be innocent until he is proved guilty.

Article 7 (1) (b) of the African charter similarly provides that: Every individual shall have the right to have his cause heard. This comprises: (b) right to be presumed innocent until proved guilty by a competent court or tribunal.

The International Covenant on Civil and Political Rights (ICCPR)[151] and UDHR equally has provision recognizing the presumption of innocence in favour of persons charged with criminal offences. Accordingly Article 14 of ICCPR provides: everyone charged with a criminal offence shall have the right to be presumed innocent until proved guilty according to law.

---

[149] See section 293 (2) ACJA 2015. The application should be ex-parte because it preserves the suit and still falls within the constitutionally permitted period for practical incarceration.

[150] Bone (ed) et al Osborn's Concise Law Dictionary 9th ed. London sweet and Maxwell 2001 p.297.

[151] The ICCPR entered into force on 23rd March 1976.

Article 11 of UDHR also provides: Everyone charged with a penal offence has the right to be presumed innocent until proved guilty according to law in public trial at which he has had all the guarantees necessary for his defence.

The import of the above provisions is that there is general presumption of innocence in favour of an accused person unless the contrary is proved in a court of competent jurisdiction. Section 145 (2) of the Evidence[152] states that whenever it is presumed that the court shall regard such fact as proved unless and until it is disproved. The burden of proving the guilt of an accused person rest on the prosecution and the standard of proof is beyond reasonable doubt.[153] In the case of *Goni v. Bornu Native Authority*[154] the court held that it is not the duty of the accused to prove his innocence, it is the duty of the accuser (prosecution to prove his guilty). This is coterminous with the case of *Bhai Chaggan Bai v State of Gujarat* [155] where the Indian Supreme Court held inter alia that:

It is a fundamental principle of criminal jurisprudence that an accused is presumed innocent. Therefore the burden lies on the prosecution to prove guilt of an accused beyond reasonable doubt... this general burden never shift and it always rest on the prosecution.

In Nigeria, there are many instances in which accused person are incarcerated in some prisons for very long periods of time without trial. Where an accused person is detained for about two years without trial, would that contravene the presumption of innocence?

In the case of *Musa and ors v. COP*,[156] the appellant were arranged before the upper area court kabong Jos, upon allegation in a first information report of commission of several offence including culpable homicide punishable with death. The appellant were detained for about 22 months. The Upper Area court refused their application for bail on the grounds of lack of jurisdiction to so do. The High court also dismissed their application for bail. On Appeal, the court of appeal held inter-alia,

---

[152] Evidence Act 2011 (amended).

[153] Ibid. section 135 (1). (see also *Musa and Anor v Cop* (2014) 9 NWLR (pt.879) 483 at P. 502, *Fayemi v Ofu* (2009) All FWLR (pt.493) 1254.

[154](1957) NWLR 40 at 42.

[155] (1964) SC 1563.

[156] Supra, pp. 448-499 para H F and P.504 para A-B Ratio 2.

that the continued detention of the appellants in prison custody for 22 month is contrary and contradictory to the age long existing principle of presumption of innocence enshrined in section 36 (5) of the 1999 constitution. Ogbauagu[157] JCA held as follows:

... it is now settled, that it is better for one hundred accused person to be punished for an offence he did not commit or had no hand in it committal. That is why the provision in section 36(5) of the 1999 constitution that every person who is charged with an offence shall be presumed innocent until he is proved guilty and this will be, beyond reasonable doubt. Happily, sentiments have no place in our courts. Thus, detention without trial when due is a gross violation of the presumption of innocence.[158]

It should be noted that a Holding charge cannot stay for over 42 days it is after the 42 limited days as prescribed by law that further incarceration would breach the presumption of innocence. It should also be noted, that the right to bail is essential to the realization of the principle of presumption of innocence provided by the constitution and African charter on Human and People's right. The court has discretion to grant bail, where it does not grant bail but instead order remanded it does not in any way violates this presumption of innocence. But where it is arbitrarily refused then it violates the presumption of innocence.[159] It is contended here that since the granting of bail is discretional and the court has the choice in respect of capital offence on either to grant bail or remand in line with the 1999[160] constitution and the ACJA[161] 2015, then the order of remand does not in any way violate the presumption of innocence[162] couple with the express fact that magistrate courts cannot grant bail for capital offence.

---

[157] Ibid p. 502.

[158] Supra.

[159] See *Obekpa v COP* (1980) NNLR 113.

[160] See Section 35 (4) of the 1999 constitution and our deliberations in chapter 3.

[161] See section 295 of the ACJA 2015 states. The court may is considering an application for remand brought before it taking into consideration the provisions of sections 158 to 188 of this Act relating to bail.

[162] Indeed the drafters of the ACJA 2015 should be applauded for aligning it with the constitution in letters and spirits. It has always been stated that the constitution cannot contradict itself.

Afterall according to justice Obaseki (JSC) in *Saidu v the State,*[163] it does not give the court any joy to se offenders escape the penalty they richly deserve but until they are proved under the appropriate law in our law court, they are entitled to walk about in our streets and tread the Nigerian soil breath the Nigeria air as free and innocent men and women while this is true, remand does not violates the presumption of innocence.

In *Bayo Johnson v Lufadeju*[164] My lord Mukhtar (delivering the lead judgment) noted that the respondent counsel raised issue 2, on whether section 263 (3) CPL was not in conflict with section 33 the 1979 constitution (and more precisely for this sub-heading section 33(5) now 36(5) dealing with presumptions of innocence).

My lord was pungent on this, and I take the liberty to reproduce him in extension:

On the presumption of innocence as laid down in section 33(5) of the constitution, I fail to see anything in the record before us that there was a contrary presumption in respect of the appellant. The appellant and his co-accused were taken before the magistrate court for the purpose of lawful remand in custody, and that was exactly what the chief magistrate did. She did not ask him of whether he was guilty or not, so the issue of his innocence didn't come to play at that stage of the proceedings. I need not go into the arguments proffered in respect of section 33(6) of the 1979 constitution supra by learned counsel for the respondents as they have been adequately covered by my reasoning's about indeed I don't think I need to belabor this issue any further, for it will be tantamount for over flogging it.

From the above statement of my lord, it is settled that Holding charge is not contrary to the presumption of innocence.

4.6. The Right to Dignity of Human Person

The dignity to the human person is rated very high in comparison with other rights. Dignity is perhaps the most fundamental attribute of an

---

[163] (1982) 4 sc 41.

[164] ibid.

individual personality and this makes it necessary that it should be protected in all circumstances.[165]

Section 34(1) of the constitution provides:

Every individual is entitled to respect for the dignity of his person and accordingly;

a. No person shall be subjected to torture or inhuman or degrading treatment.
b. No person shall beheld in slavery or servitude.
c. No person shall be required to perform forced or compulsory labour.

Similarly, Article 5 of the African charter of Human and peoples rights provides that:

Every individual shall have the right to the respect of the dignity inherent in a human being and to the recognition to his legal status. All forms of exploitation and degradation of man particularly slavery trade, torture, cruel, inhuman or degrading punishment and treatment shall be prohibited.

The wordings of these provisions are clear and unambiguous and the law is that they should be construed and given their literal interpretation.[166]

In the case of *Mr. Kingsley Ikonna v Commissioner of police Lagos State and 4 ors,*[167] the applicant was arrested by some policemen who allegedly raided a hotel to arrest a robbery suspect. In a bid to obtain a confessional statement, the applicant was arrested and taken to a detention facility and subjected to physical abuse and torture by the policemen. The court held inter-alia the fundamental rights of citizens are constitutionally guaranteed in chapter IV of the 1999 constitution, the court has duty to protect these constitutionally guaranteed rights. In the instant case, the applicant was incarcerated and subjected to severe torture. Therefore the

---

[165] See with approval the following cases *Amakir. v Iwowari* (1974)1 RSLR 5, *Mogali v Boards of custom* (1982) 3, NCLR 552 *Alabob v Boylse* (1984) % NCLR 830 *Dele Giwa v. IGP* Unrep Suit No. M/44/83 of 30/7/84 *Babli v COP* (1985) 6 NCLR 424 *HC. R. v Bodom* (1935) 2 WACA 353. *Duee v Haske* (1961) All NLR 330 SC. *Mc Nabb v. United States* 318 US332. *Mallory v United State* 354 US 449.

[166] See the case of *Traina Ltd v. Universal Trust Bank Plc* (2009) 12 NWLR (pt.1155) 313.

[167] (2010) 12 NWLR (pt.1) 365.

arrest of the applicant as well as torture and shooting while in detention and his continuous incarceration are elegant violations of the fundamental rights of the applicant as protected by section 34 and 35 of the constitution. In *Alaboh v Boyles and Anor,*[168] the beating, pushing and submersion with the applicant, head in a pool of water by the first respondent was held to constitute inhuman and degrading treatment.

A prisoner, as a result of being in prison, is particularly vulnerable to arbitrary and unlawful action. Those who are responsible for his imprisonment should be subject to the scrutiny and control of and in particular, the ordinary courts of the land.[169]

Judge Tumin's postulation is more appropriate for Nigeria considering the prejudice that follows imprisonment; the prisoner, having been neglected by society and the prison system must find some solace in the law and the courts. Accordingly, an international legal instrument[170] provides that all persons under any form of detention or imprisonment shall be treated in a human manner and with respect to the inherent dignity of the human person.

It should be noted that respect for human dignity is as a critical issue in most Nigerian prisons. This is because the fact of imprisonment appears to offer some incentive to impunity for security officers. Torture of inmates in Nigeria is norm than the exception.

Rule 8 of the UN standard minimum rules for the treatment of prisoners[171] to which Nigeria is a synatory provides as follows:

---

[168] (1984) 3 NCLR 830.

[169] His Honour judge Stephen Tumie prison Disturbances April 1990:Report of an Enquiry (1456,1991) pt 2. 11 291.

[170] United Nations Body of Principles for the protection of All persons under Any form of Detention or imprisonment, principle1-United Nations Document A/43/49 (1988). Principle 6 further declares that "cruel in human or degrading treatment should be interpreted so as extent the widest possible protection against abuses, whether physical or mental, including the holding of a determined or imprisoned person in conditions which deprive him, temporarily or permanently of the use of any of his natural services, such as sight or hearing, or his awareness of place and passing of time".

[171] Adopted by the First United Nations congress on the prevention of crime and the Treatment of offenders held at Geneva in 1955 and approved by the economic and social council by its regulations 663 (XXIV) of 31st July 1957 and 2016 (LXII) of 13th May 1977.

The different categories of prisoners shall be kept in separate institution, taking into account of their sex, age, criminal record, the legal reasons for the detention and the necessities of their treatment.[172]

However, in Nigeria, segregation of prisoners is observed more in breach despite the express provisions of section 2(4) of the prisons Act[173] to that effect.

Thus, the former Director of the Nigerian prison service (now correctional services), Mr. Lily Olo, admitted that there is a problem when he said:

> The problem of overcrowding has not only imposed strains a prison management but has rendered the concept of classification meaningless in our prison.[174]

According to D. U. Ekumankama,[175] the direct consequences of overcrowding and or congestion of prison is that even good managers are rendered helpless as there is nothing they can do on their own to solve the problem. The position as reported by the Nigeria Law Reform Commission in 1983[176] is that offenders are locked up under inhuman conditions often with 100 (hundred) inmate occupying a cell that was meant for at most 20 persons.

The paramount question to ask is how Holding charge violates the right to dignity? It is hereby contended that the issue of prison congestion is a matter of it's own which shall be dealt with latter, but does it mean that the cause of prison congestion is only Holding charge? One may simply dispose of this question by answering in the negative, but with pungent qualification that sometimes, due to the lack of diligence and vigilance by the police and courts in handling ATPS and ensuring that they are brought to court within the permitted period, the ATPS spends more number of day weeks, months or years in remand.

---

172 In adopting the above international regulation, the prisons. Regulations made pursuant to the prisons Act has in its section 15, 16 and 17 made similar provisions.

173 Prisons Act cap. P. 29 LFN 2004.

174 Lilly Olo, The state of the Nigerian prisons, being a paper delivered at the National Seminar on prison Reform June 18-20, 1990. P. 7 .

175 D. U. Ekumankeama op.cit P.228.

176 Quoted in "Behind the wall published by civil liberties organization in August, 1996 P.1.

Therefore, the improper use of Holding charge may cause prison congestion leading to violation of Dignity but where Holding is used with due diligence,[177] no issue of prison congestion would arise and no right to dignity would be violated.

4.7. The Effect of Holding Charge Practice

From the forgoing, this research work have been able to show with accurate and cogent reasons through painstaking consideration and dilation of the various provisions of the constitution and other statutes with judicial blessings on the reasons, justification and procedures of Holding charge, the research work went as far dilating on the decision of the Supreme Court it is hereby proposed to look deep into the effect of Holding charge in our criminal justice system.

However, some preliminary point need be noted before we proceed, first it is the position of the research work that Holding charge is constitutional and even a necessary evil in our criminal justice system; second, the phrase "a necessary evil means it a desired machinery of justice labeled an illegibility; Third, that the discourse on effects of Holding charge shall as a point of note be positive, and problems or issues arises when it is not properly used as permitted by law.

Consequently, this sub-heading will examine the necessary implications of this practice by the police and magistrate courts on the Speedy Administration Criminal Justice in Nigeria on the defence of the accused and on the Nigerian prison. This is because the wide goose discordant tunes about Holding charge by scholars and jurist is the obvious fact that those remanded in custody on the basis of the so called holding charge are sometimes forgotten in custody, or further investigations of the allegation against them are not accorded due attention. Such inmates sometimes remain in custody for periods longer than they would have served if they have been tried, found guilty and sentenced.

177 That is, according to the tenor of the law there would be less congestion especially if there are separate cells for different categories of inmates.

4.8. Effect on Speedy Administration of Criminal Justice in Nigeria

The improper use of Holding charge practice is one of the chief reason why criminal trial in Nigeria is largely regarded as unfair. Though, much has been said about it legality and constitutionality, the league of lawyers and scholars rather continue raining criticisms on it as a machinery, should instead research, argue propound, dilate and create a workable outfit and parastatals to ensure the strict observable of the law. Matters of this nature that deals with the Fundamental Human Rights of the suspect must be treated with full attention and facilities. Pitiably in Nigeria the reverse is the case. This is because the autonomy of the judiciary is not yet sacrosanct and strictly observe. Dr Daniel Bwala, a lawyer and chieftain of the All Progressive Ruling Congress recently said, it was selfish of the governors to continue to operate in complete disregard for the presidential executive order 10 which gives expression to the constitutionally guaranteed financial autonomy of the judiciary[178]

The right to fair hearing within a reasonable time is guaranteed by section 36 of the constitution of Nigeria (as amended). By section 36(4) of the constitution, whenever any person is charged with a criminal offence, he shall unless the charge is withdrawn, be entitled to a fair hearing in public within a reasonable time. Although, the term "reasonable" is nebulous, in section 35(5) of the same constitution the expression" a reasonable time " is defined as a period of (1) day or (2) day, or such other days as the court may consider to reasonable depending on the distance of the court and section 35(4) define 2 or 3 months for period of bail.

The implication of a community reading of the above section is that a suspect must be brought to court within a reasonable time. If it can be submitted that section 35 (4) of the constitution provides period of remand/or bail if the court so pleases, then it should not be so difficult to further submit that the meaning and import of bringing to court within a reasonable time within the spirit and letters of section 35(5) and 36 (4) maybe for purpose of remand trial and/or trial depending on the facts and

---

[178] O. Ajayi, judiciary autonomy: Govs more powerful than Buhari- APC chieftain. Vanguard, April 17,2021.

circumstances of the case. What amounts to reasonable time has been well settled by then Supreme Court, in the case of *Ariori v Elemo*[179] the court held per Obaseki JSC thus;

> "Reasonable time must mean the period of time which in the search for justice, does not wear out parties and their witnesses and which is required to ensure that justice is not only done but appears to reasonable person to be done"[180]

Now, the legal reasoning that need be done is that, is 2 or 3 months such an unreasonable time for the law to grant to a suspect on bail or on remand after making it very compulsory for the suspect to be charged to a court before 1 or 2 days or such other days (which can be for a remand proceedings or full trial depending on the facts of the case) being the time? If the above is reasonable and agreed, then the issue of Holding charge having negative effect on speedy administration of criminal justice should not even arise. Although every case has to be examined and determined on its own peculiar facts and circumstances, the American Court laid down some guiding factors to be considered in construing the delay in prosecuting an accused person. In *Baker v. Wingo*,[181] the court observes as follows:

> Some of the factors which court assess in determining whether a particular defendant has been deprived of his right. Though, some might express them in different ways, we identify for such factors, length of delays, the reason for the delay the defendant assertion of his rights and prejudice to the defendant.

It should be noted that if the machinery of Holding charge is properly used it would in turn make way for speedy trial of suspect in Nigeria, as the Supreme Court cautioned in *Dantata v Mohammed*[182] thus:

> "care must be taken to ensure that what is supposed to be a machinery of justice should not grind so slowly that persons who

---

[179] See for instance *Nnajiorfor v Ukonu* (1989)2 NWLR (pt.9) 686, at 695; *Ononyo v Aku* (1983)2.

[180] (1983) 1 SCNLR 1 at 24-28 and 15-16.

[181] See also *Isaiku Mohammed v. kano Native Anthony* (1968) 1 All NLLR 424, *Obiaso v Okoye (*1989) 5 NWLR (pt. 119) 80.

[182] 407 US 1514530 (1972).

stand to benefit by the delay will succeed in converting the machinery of justice to that of injustice".

4.8.1. The Effect on the Defense of the Accused Person

The judicial stand that it is better for 99 criminal to go unpunished than for one innocent person to be punished is one of the most human reasoning on record.[183] In this light, the 1999 constitution (as amended) in order for the accused person to have adequate facilitates for her defense provides that every person who is charged with a criminal offence shall be entitled to:

a. Be informed promptly in the language that he understands and in details of the nature of the offence;
b. Be given adequate time and facilities for the preparation of his defence
c. Defend himself in person or by his legal practitioner of his own choice;
d. Examine, in person or by his legal practitioner the witnesses called by the prosecution before any court or tribunal and obtain the attendance and carryout the examination of witnesses to testify on his behalf before the court or tribunal on the same condition as those applying to the witness called by the prosecution.

The above fundamental constitutional provisions are targeted towards ensuring that a suspect or an accused person is accorded every deserved opportunity to defend himself and prove his innocence before any court or tribunal in this country. All this juncture, it is necessary to examine some sub paragraph in section 36(6) in the whether it conflicts or not.

Section 36(6) (b) states that an accused shall be given adequate time and facilities for the preparation of his defense where an accused is remanded on a holding charge, he is normally given adequate time and facilities to prepare his case through legal practitioner of his choice, while at the same the state prepares their case. So no of conflict arises there from.

[183] (2008) SENJ. P. 17 et 25.

Further, the right of an accused person to be examine in person or by a legal practitioner of his choice, the witnesses called by the prosecution before any court or tribunal and also to obtain the attendance and carry out the examination of witness to testify on his behalf before the court or tribunal on the same conditions as those applying to the witness called by the prosecution, envisages an opportunity for the accused to collect evidence both documentary, real and oral as well as identify his witness(es) for attendance. It is submitted that, a Holding charge is filled ex-parte[184] and as such its not a full blown trial where witnesses would be required to testify and examination takes place. So all this rights do not arise.

It need be noted at this juncture that, an accused on remand practically prepares his case through his legal practitioner who is all time has free access to the accused for questioning of the facts and circumstance of the case. Little wonder why Samuel Dash[185] articulated thus:

> Without the assistance of counsel, the defendant is practically powerless to challenge the prosecution. It is the lesson of human experience that even in the case of the most well intentioned persecutors the absence of such a challenge can result in carelessness and failure to review the evidence and properly prepare the case, while makes it easier to convict the innocent.[186]

The importance of the assistance of counsel was underscored by David Fellman in the following words:

> without the assistance of counsel, most persons accused of crimes are not likely to have an adequate defence. A defendant needs a lawyer as urgently as a sick man needs a doctor and in many instances, more urgently, for while nature often heal the sick without outside aid it seems to have little concern for the plight of the accused.[187]

---

[184] *See Ukwunneyi and Anor v the state* (1989) 3 NSCC 42 at 45 per Oputa JSC.

[185] S. Dash, The Emerging Role & Function of the Criminal Defence Lawyer; North Carolina Review, April 1969, at 47.

[186] Section 36(5) of the constitution. See also Article 7 (1) (b) of the Africa charter on Human and peoples Right.

[187] Ibid at footnote 71.

It is my humble opinion that no right is breached or violated due to the instrumentality of Holding charge. This is because while in remand he have a right to legal representation which would not refused by any authority, it is to be noted that the court must view every case on it own merit, and must desist the temptation of labeling what is legal/illegal due to some unascertained and disproved facts of perceived violation of rights. Therefore, as Justice kayode Eso JSC admonished:

> ... it is the function of judges to keep the law alive in motion and to make it progressive for the purpose of arriving at the end of justice without being inited by technicalities to find every conceivable and acceptable way of avoiding narrowness that would spell foe, a judge must possess an aggressive stance in integrity the law.[188]

4.8.2. The Effect on Nigerian Prison

The prison inmates consist of both those awaiting trial and those convicted of various offences. However, in most cases as we can see later, the awaiting trial immates in prisons outnumber those already convicted. We must also note that those awaiting trial are and remain innocent until they are convicted by a court or tribunal for committing an offence under the law.

According to Showunmi,[189] an awaiting trial person (ATP) is someone remanded by an order of a court or tribunal in prison custody in order to ensure his availability before the detaining authority in due course for the hearing of the case to prove or establish his innocence or guilt. Awaiting trial person population and many factors are responsible for it, among which is the police practice of Holding charge without due diligence.

Holding charge are one of the causes of the large number of awaiting trial inmates in Nigerian prisons and as such a major source of congestion of prisons. Over congestion of prisons in Nigeria is extremely acute. Both convicted prisoners and those awaiting trial are all dumped better in small

---

[188] See also the dictum of Oputa JSC in *Josiah v. the state* (1985) ! NWLR pt ! p 131 at P.140 see also *Okoduna v the state* (1993) NWLR (pt. 283) p. 208.

[189] *Transbridge co ltd v Survey international Ltd* (1986) NWLR (pt. 37) P.576 at 596.

cells. The greater proportions of prisoners in Nigeria prisons are those awaiting trial, remanded by court orders.[190]

Those remanded by the order of the courts recounted for about sixty seven percent of prison population. Due to mainly administrative reasons such as lack of transportation to take the person to court; absence of counsel, unwillingness of the magistrate to go on with the case because of lack of jurisdiction, many of these remand prisoner remain in prison for prolonged period of time without trial[191] consequently, the prisoners are incarcerated indefinitely under harsh and inhuman conditions even where they have not been found guilty.[192]

The Civil Liberties Organization has described the condition of Nigerian prisons in the following words:

> Behind the wall of practically every prison in Nigeria is slum where men and women too literally live on top of each other. From prison to prison the housing conditions consistency reveal themselves to be wretched and in human.[193]

In line with the above, Hon. Justice Alhasssan Idoko of blessed memory had in 1981[194] said:

> They reveal a complete picture of dehumanizing conditions. Convicts and even those awaiting trial are caged and cramped together in cells meant for either only one person or fewer person than are hoarded there. The sloppings (sic) and stench all around defy solution and the considerable regimentation throughout the period of the prison sentence has less of a therapeutic value.

The report given by Civil Liberties Organization (CLO) on the sanitary conditions of the Nigerian prisons is relevant in this context. The report states:

---

[190] L. A Showunmi, "Reform of Criminal Justice system and congestion of prisons by awaiting trial persons; Are there alternative? Paper presented at the summit of stakeholders on the Administration of justice in Lagos on 17th June 2004.

[191] T.O. Ifaturot "Nigerian prisoners and the Human Rights Campaigns: some challenges". Nigerian current law review. 1994, p.87.

[192] Civil liberties organisation Annual Report in Nigeria 1999 at P.200.

[193] Taofile Adedamada, Op.cit at P.289.

[194] See Behind the Wall, A report on prisons conditions in Nigeria and Nigerian prison system. CLO. 1976 Edition P.13.

> The state of sanitation and hygiene in the prison was quite appaling. Water shortage was acute. Inmates were usually unable to take their baths for several days and had even access to water for washing clothes. Toileteries were a luxury. Bed bugs, cockroaches, rats and mosquitoes bred freely. Ventilation was poor because most cells either had no window at all or their windows were sealed in an attempt to prevent prison escapes.[195]

Prof. Fagbohun said:

> In a report by the National Burean of statistics (NBS), covering data from 2011 to 2015, it was reported that up to 72.5% of Nigeria's total prison population are inmates serving term while awaiting trials. The National human right commission also reported earlier in a 2014 report that 70% of the inmates in prison across the country are awaiting trial. The same report confirmed that the "total prison population in Nigeria in 56,718 comprising 17,686 convicts (4,000 lifers; 1612 condemned convicts) and 39,032 awaiting trial persons. In addition, the vanguard Newspaper of 14th January, 2017 reported that no fewer than 47,817 inmates are currently awaiting trial in Nigeria prison out of a total number of 62,200 detainees. It should also be noted that, while congestion is an issue that constantly attracts attention in Nigeria in criminal justice discourse, little or no attention is paid to the congestion of police calls and the ways and manner in which the police deal with the congestion.

Thus, Jiti Ogunye[196] observed that owing to poor crime intelligence gathering police officers usually commence their investigation after affecting arrests, and this account for congestion in police cells. He went further to state that arrest are made at the beginning of investigation by the police and advised that pre-arrest intelligence can help in limiting the number of days in which criminal suspects are kept in police custody.

The Executive Summary of 2012 Audit Report carried out by the National Human Rights Commission in collaboration with the Legal Resources Consortium revealed that during the exercise, it was discovered

---

[195] See Behind the wall, ibid and quoted in ignatus . Ayube, "Towards a more appropriate. Sentiency policy in Nigeria "in Nigerian legal reform journey No.3, January, 1983 P.22.
[196] Jiti Ogunye, Criminal Justice System in Nigeria: The imperative of plea bargaining, lawyers' league for Human Rights, August 2005, p. 29.

most of the prisons here congested. The congestion was as a result of the number of inmates that were awaiting trial. Comparatively, in all the 173 prisons audited across the country, the lockup was 50,645 compared to a capacity of 46, 024.

The analysis by the zones revealed the following results below:

S/N	ZONE	CAPACITY	LOCKUP
1	South South	7,298	10,232
2	North East	9,011	6,677
3	North Central	7,772	6,816
4	South West	7,722	11,078
5	North West	9,754	8,087
6	South East	4,467	7,664
Total		46,024	50,645

Across the prisons, the number of Awaiting trial inmates was far above that of convicts. In 173 prisons audicted, out of 50, 645 lockups. The number of convicts was 13,901 compared to awaiting trial inmates 35,889. Besides the awaiting trial inmates, Ikom prison in Cross River had 5 lodgers, Ahoada prison in River State and Benin prison in Edo State had 2 and 1 lodgers respectively. (Lodgers are persons kept imprison without order of court detaining them. There are no records of such inmates in the prison records).

In Ikoyi Prison, they were 221 convicts as against 1574 ATMs, while Abeokuta New and Akure had 63 convicts each compared to 425 and 644 ATMs respectively. Also, Goron Dutse prison in Kano State had 877 ATMs and 350 convicts, while MSP Gusua in Zamfara state had 154 convicts and 515 ATMs. The situation is not different in Enugu prison which had 1,453 ATMs as against 172 convicts and Owerri had 1,602 ATMS and 143 convicts. Port Harcourt prisons had 121 convicts and 2,607 ATMs while Calabar with 93 convicts had 600 ATMs. Similarly, Ugwashi-Uku prison in Delta had 64 convicts and 511 ATMs.

Further, in Jalingo prison, there were 320 ATMs, compared to 95 convicts; 647 ATMs as against 173 convicts in Bauchi prison and 322 ATMs as against 186 convicts in Yola prison.

The number of inmates on Holding charge were 11,047 nationwide. In the South East zone, 2526 were on holding charge with Owerri prison holding 1,179 of the category of inmates. Furthermore, in North East

Zone, about 465 inmates were on holing charge. 300 of this category of inmates were found in Bauchi prison. In the South West Zone, they were 1154 with 330 found in Medium prison Akure, 4,914 were found in the South-South Zone, with 2543,811,469 in Port Harcourt, MSP Oko, and Ugwashi-Uku respectively. Similarly, in the North West Zone, they were 1600, with 795 found in Kano prison, while North central, they were 368 inmates on holding charge. This was due to the executive summary of 2012 prison Audit Report.[197]

More recently on 18th October 2017,[198] it was reported that over eight hundred inmates in Nigeria prisons, Cross River State command were awaiting trial. The state comptroller of the Nigerian Prison Service (NPS), Mr. Imaikpo Ndaekon disclosed this while paying a visit to the state governor, Prof. Ben. Ayade. He said the state has six formations which were operation above capacity. A total 854 of 1, 154 inmates were awaiting trial, while 254 were convicted, with 46 condemned he said. He continued thus, "of this number, 32.7 percent were charged for murder, 27.7 percent for armed robbery, 8.9 percent for ordinary robbery, 5 percent for unlawful possession of fire arms, 20.2 percent for ordinary stealing, 4.3 percent for assault and 1.2 percent for other offences".

Similarly, the Nigeria 2019 Human Right s Reports[199] released an executive report to the effect that lengthy pretrial detention remained a serious problem. According to NCS figures released in July 2019, 68 percent of the prison population consisted of detainees awaiting trial, often for years.

Interestingly, the Bureau of Democracy, Human Rights and Labor[200] released an Executive Summary on the 3oth March, 2021. It was reported that over crowding was a major problem in prisons. That, although the total designed capacity of the country's prisons was 50, 153 inmates as of October 2020 prison facilities held 64, 817 prisoners. Approximately, 74

---

[197] Executive summary of 2012 Prison Audit Report.

[198] Over 800 inmates awaiting trail in Cross River prisons 18th oct, 2017. Barrister Ng. Com < https://barrister ng.com/800-inmates-awating-trial-cross-river-prison/>accessed 4th May, 2021.

[199] Nigeria 2019 Human Rights Reports. Executive Summary.

[200] 2020 Cpuntry Reports on Human Rights Practices: Nigeria https://www.state.gov/reports/2020-country-reports/on-human-rights-practices/nigeria/accessed on 4th May, 2021.

percent of inmates were in pretrial detention or remanded. In December 2019, according to press reports five inmates awaiting trial at Ikoyi prison were accidentally electrocuted in their cell due to over crowding.

Chapter Five

Summary/Conclusion and Recommendations

5.1. Summary

The research have been to able lay bare the meaning, reasons, procedures, justifications and legality of Holding Charge in relation to extent laws.[201] The research also dabbled into the effects of Holding charge on the rights of suspects, and the rights are sacred and fundamental in our *corpus juris* Nigerian. The research also, in view of the improper use of the machinery, discussed on the effects on speedy administration of criminal justice in Nigeria, effect on the defence of the accused person and even the Nigerian prisons (now correctional centers).

For purposes of summary, it is proposed to reflect on the ordeals of *Sikiru Alade* and *Hyginus Ajibo*[202] which amplify the real concerns that may result from the pre-trial remand order that is not followed up by the remanding judge/magistrate, the prison officials and other persons upon whom obligation to so do are vested.

Sikiru Alade was a panel beater in Lagos before his arrest on 9th March, 2003. He was arrested by a plain cloth police man in mufti who at the time of the arrest did not disclose his identity. He was forcefully dragged to Ketu Police Station where he was detained. Six days later (15th May, 2013), he was taken to the Magistrates Court, and by way of a holding charge on an allegation of armed robbery. The magistrate ordered his remand in kirikiri maximum prison in Apapa, Lagos. Alade was not returned to the court or any court of competent jurisdiction and therefore remained remanded in prison for 9 years, 6 months without a trial or a

---

[201] Administration of Criminal Justice Act 2015 and 1999 Constitution as amended.

[202] Extracted from Prof. Fagbohun's, supra.

formal charge before any court. The an application was brought on his behalf at the ECOWAS Court of Justice as *Sikuru Alade v Federal Republic of Nigeria.*[203] The court handed down its judgment on 11th June 2012, and held that *Alade's* detention for almost 10 years without a trial or charge violated his rights under the African charter on Human and people's Rights. The Chief Judge of Lagos eventually ordered his release on 18th September, 2012.

Again, *Hyginus Ajibo* was accused of murder. He was arrested and remanded in custody in 1997 where he spent the first three years. In the year 2000, he was charged to Enugu High Court where commencement of his trial got stuck. He spent approximately 16 years from the day of his remand in prison Custody without trial. On 17th February, 2014 the High Court granted him bail pending the determination of his trial.

Upon the two cases above, it is safe to submit by way of summary that the entire research tends to avoid the event that occurred in the course of prosecution of *Sikiru* and *Ajibo*, and rather calls for a proper and diligent use of Holding Charge, having established its legality.

5.2. Conclusion

The whole gamut of the research is geared towards the aim of justifying the use of Holding Charge and salvaging it from the many criticisms it has suffered in the Nigerian legal system.

It should be noted that a critical examination of the subject matter portray the level of judicial activism of the courts[204] in Nigeria, it also goes along way to appraise the fecundity of the legislature in Nigeria; starting from the Lagos state legislative house that deemed it fit to embark on a law reform for this purpose, the National Assembly and Legal Consensus on the subject matter. The use of Holding Charge is a machinery *siu generis* which came into practice engendered by the need to create a balance in the course of a criminal prosecution falling within the circumstances.

It should be parenthetically noted that Holding Charge is very important because it concerns certain fundamental Human Rights which

[203] Eckul/CCJ/APP/05/11.

[204] Specifically the Supreme Court.

when violated may cause grave danger to the case of the prosecution, therefore the need for a proper study of the subject matter cannot be over emphasized.[205] Accordingly, it has duly been established that the practice is not illegal and that the necessity of the subject matter is due to the standard of our Criminal Administration System which is not near perfect.

It should be noted however, the proper use of Holding Charge cannot lead to a violation of Fundamental Human Right, therefore there is grave need for proper literatures to be written in respect of the subject matter. Seminars, conference and more papers should be written to explore this bitter truth in our legal system. The negative effects of the subject matter is so grave, hence the need for it's proper use.

It can be comfortably submitted that, by the combine effect of sections 293-299 of the Administration of Criminal Justice Act and Section 35 (5 and 4) of the 1999 constitution, Holding charge although not expressly mentioned in the constitution or any law, is practicable in reality.

Little wonder why *Prof. Fagbehun*[206] submitted thus,

> The bulk of the challenges confronting the use of holding charges and pre trial remands stems not so much from the presumption that holding charge and pre-trial remands, ab-initio, violate constitutionally guaranteed rights. Rather, they relate more to the challenges and inefficiency that have characterized the administration of Criminal Justice System in Nigeria. Some of these challenges include deliberate and negligent abandonment of pre-trial suspects in prison custody which ultimately results to prison congestion, lack of follow up of remand cases by remanding judges/magistrates as required by the law; lack of or poor investigation of criminal allegations by police officers, before application for remand orders, among others.

5.3. Recommendation

It is without doubts that there are already existing blueprints, reports and well research opinions and recommendations in our Criminal Justice

[205] In 1945 the U.N realized and expressed in her charter that the future peace of the world depended on the guarantee to every man, woman and child of certain fundamental human right and freedoms.

[206] ibid.

System while it is common knowledge that our laws in this regard may not have reached its very best, what appears to be more deficient is not really the law but the machineries through which our criminal justice is administered. The law has taken some steps with some laudable provisions to ensure that a person brought to court by way of holding charge and remanded in prison custody is given serious monitoring to ensure his or her case does not end up like that of *Sikiru Alade or Hyginus Ajibo.*

The above notwithstanding, the following recommended should be considered

1. The should be strict adherence by remanding magistrates and high court judges to the provisions of the constitution. ACJA 2015 and ACJL 2011 on proper and continuing monitoring of suspects who have been placed on remand by court orders.
2. The chief judge or chief magistrate as the case maybe, should play a supervisory role on remanding judges and magistrates. In addition to their judicial functions, remanding judges and magistrate should file monthly reports to be submitted to the Chief Judge of each state on the number of suspects remanded in prison custody, the dates the orders will lapse, and the necessary follow-ups to be done by prosecutors, the Attorney General or the Director of public prosecution before the next adjourned date.
3. Monthly or bi-monthly visit by the chief judge or designated judge or chief magistrate to prisons to take inventory of suspects in prison custody whose date's of remand have lapsed, but are still in custody awaiting trial or formal charge. Diligent steps should be taken as these will reveal the like's of Sikiru Alode and Hyginus Ajibo who lan quished in custody awaiting trial or formal charge before a court of competent jurisdication.
4. The legal departments in the respective police divisional offices should be formally saddled with responsibility to follow up with police prosecutors on remand cases. The Departments should ensure as a matter of utmost importance that proper preliminary police investigation is carried out before taking any suspect to court for remand. Disciplinary measure should be imposed on any officer or police prosecutor found to have acted in contravention

of laid down rules and guidelines before applying for remand orders.

5. Criminal investigation departments of anti -graft agencies and offices of directors of public prosecutions of ministries of justice across the country should also be formally saddled with the responsibility to compile a list of remand, cases bi-monthly or on monthly basis, and forward same to the relevant Attorney-General, for appropriate action as provided for under the constitution.
6. Comptrollers of prisons should equally be formally mandated to take and keep records of remand cases and forward same to the comptroller general of prisons who in turn will make it available to chief judges of federal and State High Courts and Chief Magistrates for appropriate action as provided for under the constitution.
7. Happily by Virtue of Section 106 of the ACJA 2015 which has been domesticated in various state's and the Nigerian Police Act 2020, it is only a police who is a legal Practitioner that can institute criminal proceedings, therefore, the expectation is that, the improper use of Holding is suppose to change since all prosecutors must now qualify as a legal practitioner who have been well trained and abreast with the law.

Bibliography

Books

Asein, J. O. Introduction to Nigerian Legal System, Lagos, Aba Press Ltd 205.

Denning, Lord. Freedom under the Law (1949)

Ese, Malemi the Nigerian Constitution of Law, Lagos, Aba Press Ltd 2005.

Fell man, D. The Defendants Rights to day, the University of Wisconsin Press. 1976.

Nwadiolo, F. The Criminal Procedure in Nigeria. Afro orbis publishing co. lLtd Nsukka 2000.

Nwazuoke, A. N. Introduction to Human Rights Law. Abakaliki, Copycraft International Human Right in context 2000, 2nd Edition, Oxford England.

Odinkalu, A. C. & Ehonwa L. Behind the wall. A Report on prison Conditions in Nigeria and the Nigerian prison system, 1991, C. L. O Lagos.

Okpara, O. Human Rights Law and Practice in Nigeria, Enugu Chengles Ltd, 2005.

Osita Eze Human Rights in Africa, selected Problems. Lagos, Macmillan Publishers 1984.

Richard Stone, Textbook on Civil Liberty. Blackstone press Ltd. London Publishers, 1994.

Wade, E. C. S. Law of the Consitution 10 ed.

Waldron R. J and other, The Criminal Justice System: An introduction. London, K & M publishers INC, Routlege, 2010.

Journals/Articles

Abdullahi, I "The Supreme Court of Nigeria decision in Lufadeju v Johnson Case 2007 8 WNR pt 1037 pg 535-whetehr unconstitutionality of holding charge in Nigeria? Journal of Law, Policy and Globalization vol. 29, 2014.

Achara, R. A. C. Justice According to Law and Due process: A Glance at two of Justice Akpabio's Decisions. Unizik Law Journal, Vol. $ NO. 1.

Adedamola, T. The Police and Holding Charge Syndrome; Issues and Challenges; Nigerian Bar Journal, 2003.

Adedeji, A. Bail and Pretrial detention: pertinent considerations under the administration of Criminal Justice legislation National Judicial institute 2019.

Adeyemi, A. "Penal Reform in Nigeria: paper submitted for publication in a new judicial order; Essays in Honour of Justice Akinola Aguda (Unpublished).

Adeyemi, A. The Criminal Justice Administration in Nigeria in the Context of the African charter on Human and Administration in Nigeria in the context of the African charter on Human and People's Rights, in Kalu & Osibanjo (Eds.) Perspective on Human Rights 1992.

Agbakoba, O. Criminal Justice Reform and Challenge of Holding Charge.

Agbakoba, O. Travesty of Justice; An Advocacy Manual Against Holding Charge. Hurlaws 2009.

Aguda, T. A. The challenges for Nigeria Law & the Nigerian Lawyer in the 21st Century. A Nigerian National Merit Award Lecture, Presented on September 14, 1988.

Akinyede, GBA. The Barr , the police and the judiciary. Nigeria Law Journal (1958) Vol. 1, No.2.

Annual Report 1994, A Civil Liberties Organization Report on the State of Human Right in Nigeria.

Dash, S. The Emerging Role & Function of the Criminal Defence Lawyer. North Carolina Review, 1969.

Dele, P. The place of the Holding Charge in Nigerians Criminal Jurisprudence, Nigerian Current Legal Problems (1996-1998) Vol 4&5.

His Honour Judge Stephen Tumie Prison Disturbances, April 1990s : Report of an Enquiry: (1456, 1991).

Ibrahim, A. Decongestion of Nigerian Prisons: an examination of the role of the Nigerian police in the application of the holding charge procedure in relation to pre-trial detainees. African Human Right Law Journal 2019.

Ifaturoti, T. O. Nigeria prisoners and the Human Rights Campaigns, some challenges. Nigerian Current Law Review 1994.

Igwe, C.A. A Legal Review of the Administration of Criminal Justice in the magistrate Court of Ebnyi State; Ebonyi State University Law Journal (2011) No. 4 No. 1.

Jiti Ogunye, Criminal Justice System in Nigeria, the imperative of plea Bargaining, Lawyers league for Human Rights 2005.

Nail McDermott; opening address to the International Conference on Human Rights Education in Rural Environments. Lagos 1985.

Nnamani JSC, "Contemporary Nigeria and Practice of Law paper presented at the 1990 Annual Conference of the NBA in Benin from 27-31 August 1990.

Ohonbamu, O. The Delima of Police Organization: under a Federal System: The Nigerian Example Nigerian Law Journal 1972 Vol. 6. No.1

Ojo, A. Fundamental Human Rights in Nigeria, the 1963 & 1979 Constitutional Provisions. Nigerian Journal of Contemporary Law. 1977-1980.

Showunmi, L. A. Reform of Criminal Justice System congestion of prisons by A. J. P's . Are there Alternative? Paper presented at there form of criminal justice summit organized by the Lagos State Ministry of Justice from 16th-17th June 2004.

Towards a Humane Prison System" submissions by the Civil liberties organization to the Nigeria Human Rights Commission, July 1996.

Yekeni, A. O. Remand Proceedings and the Rights to personal liberty in Nigeria: Revisiting Supreme Court decision in Lufadeju's case. Lagos State University Law Journal 2011/2012.

Papers

2020 Country Report on Human Rights Practices: Nigeria. Executive summary

Executive Summary of 2012 Prison Audit Report.

Fagbohun, O. A. Holding Charge and Remand in Prison Custody Prior to trial: An Agenda for Urgent Reforms. Being a text of lecture Delivered at the 1st Annual Law Week of the Nigerian Barr. Association, Epe Branch, in Honour of Honourable Mr. Justice G. A. Oguntade, JSC FNIALS, CFR on 25th April, 2017.

Falana, F. Constitutional validity of pre-charge detention of suspects. February 9th 2016

Lily, O. The state of the Nigerian Prisons being a paper delivered at the national seminar on prison reform June 18-20,1990.

Nigeria 2019 Human Rights Report. Executive summary, July 2019.

Over eight hundred inmates awaiting trial in Cross River Prisons 18th October, 2017.

Ozekhome, M. A holding charge is patently illegal under the constitution (part 1) premium times Dec 19th, 2015.

Internet

<http://hur/laws.org/prison-reform>

<http://Lagosministryofjustice.ord>

<http://www.seribd.bm/document/54726488/criminaljustice-Reform-Article-Article>

<https//ACR.org.21/resource-central/chief-Justice-of-Nigeria-criticizes-use-of-holding-charge>

<Https://pal.law/travesty-justice-advocacy-manual-against-holding-charge.2004/

<https://Thenigerialawyer.com/constitutional-validity-of-pre-charge-detention-of-suspects-by-femi-falana/>.

<Https://Www.Dn/Partner.Com/Holding-Statutory-Constitution-Basis-Nigeria Prof Fagbohun/>

<https://www.premiumtimeorg.com/features-and-interviews/195426-a-holding-charge-is-patently-illegAZal-under-the-constitution-apart1.html.

https://barristerng.com/800-inmates-awiting-trial-cross-river-prison/.

Newspapers

Guardian News paper on today, July 15, 2004.

Premium time December 19th, 2015.

Vanguard New Paper of April 17, 2021.

NOTE: THIS PROJECT WAS WRITTEN IN 2020, IN PARTIAL FULFILMENT OF THE REQUIREMENTS TO BE AWARDED LL.B (HONS) DEGREE IN LAW, UNIVERSITY OF CALABAR, CALABAR.

FOR MORE INFO ON THE AUTHOR, SEND MESSAGES TO – mbangconfidence714@gmail.com, and morelaw6@gmail.com.

www.ingramcontent.com/pod-product-compliance
Lightning Source LLC
LaVergne TN
LVHW010719210926
848485LV00008B/1455/J
9781680535693